ENGINEERING PROJECTS FOR YOUNG SCIENTISTS

Revised Edition

Richard C. Adams
and
Peter H. Goodwin

FRANKLIN WATTS
A Division of Scholastic Inc.,
New York ▪ Toronto ▪ London ▪ Auckland ▪ Sydney ▪
Mexico City ▪ New Delhi ▪ Hong Kong
Danbury, Connecticut

Photographs ©: Cohn & Wolfe/Courtesy of Intel: 105; David Sailors: 23; Fundamental Photos/Richard Megna: 78; Peter Arnold Inc./Leonard Lessin: 44, 84; Photo Researchers, NY: 25 (George Haling), 66 (Alexander Lowry); PhotoEdit: 13 (Michael Newman), 40 (D. Young-Wolff); Stock Boston: 16 (Elizabeth Hamlin), 29 top (Kent Knudson); Stone: cover (Glen Allison), 6 (Jeff Corwin), 50 (Robin Smith); Superstock, Inc.: 29 bottom, 53, 73; The Image Works: 35 (Gontier), 10 (Network Prod.), 24 (M. Siluk); The Stock Shop/Tom Tracy: 36.

NOTE TO READERS:

Throughout this book, most measurements are given only in metric units because that is the system of measure used by most professional scientists. Words in *italics* appear in the Glossary at the back of this book.

Adams, Richard C. (Richard Crittenden)
    Engineering projects for young scientists/Richard C. Adams and Peter H. Goodwin.—Rev. Ed.
    p.   cm.—(Projects for young scientists) Rev. ed. of: Engineering projects for young scientists / Peter H. Goodwin.
    Includes bibliographical references and index.
    Summary: Presents practical problems and science fair projects related to engineering and physics, covering such subjects as force, friction, motion, sound waves, light waves, and mechanics.
    ISBN 0-531-11668-9 (lib. bdg.)
    1. Engineering—Experiments—Juvenile literature. 2. Physics—Experiments—Juvenile literature. [1. Engineering—Experiments. 2. Physics—Experiments. 3. Experiments.] I. Goodwin, Peter, 1951– . II. Goodwin, Peter, 1951– . Engineering projects for young scientists. III. Title. IV. Series.
TA149.A33   2000
620'.0078—dc21   99-30418
                                                CIP

©1987, 2001 Franklin Watts, a division of Scholastic Inc.
All rights reserved. Published simultaneously in Canada.
Printed in the United States of America.
1 2 3 4 5 6 7 8 9 10 R 10 09 08 07 06 05 04 03 02 01

C O N T E N T S

PHYSICS AND ENGINEERING: HOW THEY'RE RELATED

Physics is the study of how matter and energy interact. It explains why things are the way they are. Physics can tell you why an apple falls to the ground when it falls off a tree or why you hear a beautiful melody when someone plays a flute. Physicists study how objects behave under various conditions.

Engineering involves the use of physical principles to solve specific problems. Engineers design bridges that cross raging rivers and find ways to make machines work more efficiently. Most people use cars without thinking much about why they are built in a particular way. However, before a car is built, engineers apply the laws of physics to its design. Before any idea becomes reality, someone has to "engineer" it.

It is an engineer's job to find the best solution to a particular problem. Although engineers usually rely on

When engineers design the interiors of automobiles, they consider features such as space and comfort.

scientific laws as they develop designs, they sometimes find ways to make things work even though they can't explain the underlying principle. For example, engineers build automobile engines even though they don't know exactly how gas burns inside the engine. An engineer's knowledge goes only so far. That is why engineering requires experimentation as well as a knowledge of science.

You may not realize it, but you have probably acted like an engineer. Have you ever played with blocks? As you placed the blocks on top of one another, you found that adding blocks in certain ways made the pile tumble to the floor. However, if you added blocks in other ways, you could build structures as tall as yourself. You experimented, you learned some basic physics, and then you applied what you learned.

Physicists sometimes use big fancy words, but you don't need to know them all to understand simple physical principles. However, as your observations and experiments become increasingly involved, more precise words may help describe what you see more clearly. Knowing more about physics also allows you to investigate things more quickly and reach more accurate conclusions.

Engineers sometimes use long, complicated mathematical equations. Math is a tool that scientists use to understand the physical world, but you can understand a lot of physics without being a math whiz. Only a few of the projects in this book require more than basic math. If you need help in this area, talk to a math or physics teacher.

This book outlines the proper method for finding answers to questions about the physical world and describes the engineering challenges related to each topic. As you complete the projects, you will learn to ask the right questions, design experiments, and build various kinds of devices. Each chapter contains a variety of related projects with background material to help you understand the experiments. After you have completed a project, this book will help you draw conclusions based on your data.

Some of the experiments can be performed quickly and are suitable for classroom science projects. Others take more time, so you may have to work on them after school, on weekends, or during school vacations. Many of the projects are appropriate for science contests or fairs, provided that you conduct the experiments in a scientifically acceptable fashion. Of course, you can do a project for any purpose you wish, provided you have the time, the inclination, and the ability.

As you work on the projects described in this book, keep in mind that they won't always work the first time you try them. When a project doesn't work, think about what might have gone wrong. A single, careless mistake sometimes leads to large problems. Keep in mind that you can learn a great deal from your mistakes. Sometimes they lead to unexpected discoveries.

Now that you have some idea of what you're in for, it's time to find a project that interests you and start working on it. Oh, one more thing—don't forget to have fun!

WORKING
SCIENTIFICALLY

Scientists and engineers choose problems that interest them and try to find solutions. To do this, they ask questions and perform experiments. Although scientists and engineers work in different ways on different problems, they always use the same process. This process is called the *scientific method.* It involves asking a question, developing a *hypothesis*, gathering data, and then trying to answer the question. This is similar to the way that most people go about solving a problem.

When you played with blocks, you may have developed hypotheses without even realizing it. You may have thought, "If I place this block on top of that block in a certain way, the structure will not fall over." To test your hypothesis, you added a block to the pile. If the blocks did not fall over, you had enough data to support the hypoth-

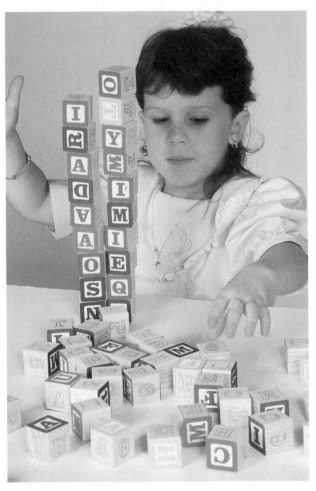

A child playing with building blocks places
a block on top of a tall pile in the hope
that the blocks will not fall over.

esis. However, if the structure crashed to the floor, the hypothesis was false. You noted whether the experiment succeeded or failed and used this information as you continued to build structures with the blocks.

As you work on the projects in this book, you will form and test hypotheses of your own. The data you collect will either support your hypotheses or lead you to reject them.

You must make sure that you are really testing what you want to test. For instance, if you want to find out whether crouching over your bicycle's handlebars will make you go down a hill faster, you need to do two test runs. First you should ride down the hill sitting upright. Then you should ride down the hill crouched over the handlebars. When you compare the length of time each run takes, you will have your answer.

However, keep in mind that your results will be meaningful only if you ride down the same hill on the same bicycle and use the same stopwatch to record the time. For the best results, the weather and the wind should also be identical during both runs. To get accurate data, only one thing—or variable—can be different. In this case, the variable is your position—upright or crouched over.

Remember that you will not be able to accept or reject your hypothesis unless your experiment yields a sufficient quantity of accurate data. Not only do you need to make *qualitative* observations, but you also need to make *quantitative* measurements to answer the question completely.

For example, some experiments may require you to measure time to the nearest minute, while others might require you to measure time to the nearest one-hundredth of a second. How precisely do you need to measure the time required to go down the hill on the bicycle? Can you obtain good enough data with a stopwatch that measures time to the nearest second, or do you need one that is more precise? You can use a Texas Instruments calculator connected to a *photogate* to make a very portable and extremely accurate timer, but before you go to the trouble of setting it up, ask yourself an important question, "Is such precision really necessary?"

Finally, keep in mind that you can never "prove" a hypothesis. As you perform additional experiments, you may find it necessary to change or modify your hypothesis so that it is more precise. As you refine your hypothesis, it will become increasingly accurate.

As you conduct experiments, make careful measurements. Record the data in a notebook so that all your results are together in one place. Make sure you write down the date and time you perform each experiment. Some scientists and inventors have been awarded patents worth a lot of money because their lab notebooks had dates proving when they had done an important experiment.

Using a word-processing program on a computer can make it easier to convert your notes into a report later. Many programs allow you to perform calculations as soon as you enter data onto a spreadsheet. Using a spreadsheet makes it easier to keep data neat and allows you to graph numbers as you get them. To obtain more information about spreadsheets, see the Appendix at the back of this book.

After you collect data, you must determine the significance of your results. This can become quite mathematical, and for some experiments you may need the assistance of someone familiar with statistics to determine whether your numbers have any real meaning.

If you analyze your data and find that you cannot reach any conclusions based on them, you may have to redesign your experiment and start over. After you have run the experiment once, you will have a better idea of the kind of data you need. This should help you redesign the experiment.

When you have come to a conclusion about your hypothesis, you might discover that your results raise more questions than they answer. Consider the bicycle experiment. Would a different bicycle give the same results? Does the steepness of the hill matter? Does the wind or the *weight* of the rider influence the outcome of your experiment?

As you can see, results from one experiment may lead to other experiments. This is true of scientific research in general. However, at some point, you must make your project presentable to an audience. This is just as true for professional scientists as it is for students.

For a student, the presentation may involve showing the apparatus, graphs, photographs, and written results at a science fair. You may also find it useful to build a scale model. Engineers create models to show how a machine

An architect finishes constructing
a scale model of a building.

will work in a real-world situation. Models are less expensive than full-scale machines, so it is possible to test more designs for your money.

Using models presents some problems, though. A model may not behave exactly like the actual machine. For example, when engineers in the movie industry use models, they have to pay special attention to time. If an engineer builds a spaceship one-tenth its normal size, it must move 100 times more slowly to act the way the real object would. To find out why, look at the following equation:

$$d = v_i t + \frac{1}{2} g t^2$$

In this equation, d is the distance, v_i is the initial *velocity* of the object, g is the *acceleration* due to gravity, and t is the time. Notice that time in the third term is squared. An object 10 times smaller than normal must move 100 times more slowly than normal to appear realistic. So while using models can be extremely helpful, it can also be a little bit tricky. For this reason, you must be careful in drawing conclusions based on models.

A science fair is an ideal opportunity to show off your project and have it judged by professionals, perhaps even by a scientist or engineer whose interests parallel yours. What an honor it would be to participate in such a competition! (See Chapter 8 to find out more about science fairs.) But before you can even hope of winning a science fair, you need to begin experimenting. That's where this book can be helpful, so read it and try any projects that interest you.

CHAPTER 2

BUILDING BRIDGES

Bridges serve many functions and are made from many materials. Some bridges cross streams, rivers, or wetlands, while others are built over highways or railroad tracks. Bridges made of a few logs or wooden planks are perfect for walking across small streams, but much more complex bridges of stone or steel are needed to span mighty rivers.

Some of the oldest bridges in the world today were built by the ancient Romans. These bridges consisted of a series of stone arches. In the last 100 years, engineers have designed and built a variety of impressive suspension bridges over wide bodies of water. The Golden Gate Bridge over San Francisco Bay, which connects Marin County, California, to the city of San Francisco, is 4,200 feet (1,280 meters) long. More than 41 million vehicles cross this bridge each year. On the opposite end of the

The Golden Gate Bridge, a suspension bridge, began carrying automobiles across San Francisco Bay in 1937.

United States, the 3,500-foot (1,100-m)-long George Washington Bridge crosses the Hudson River, connecting New York City with Fort Lee, New Jersey. More than 52 million vehicles pass over this bridge each year.

No matter where a bridge is built or what it is made of, it allows people to travel over some obstacle. The design of the bridge and the materials from which it is made depend on its location, how it will be used, and what kinds of construction materials are readily available. Engineers who design and build bridges must understand *mechanics*—the study of *force* and motion.

A SIMPLE BRIDGE

What You Need	
Four C-clamps	Trowel
50 pieces of knot-free wood, 0.5 × 5 × 60 centimeters	Ruler
	Bathroom scale
Two tables	Four small blocks of wood, 5 cm on each side
Light rope, 1 meter	
Two buckets, 20-liter size	Table saw
Enough sand to fill one bucket	Drill and drill bits

Have you ever walked across an old wooden floor that seemed "springy"? Today, wooden floors are generally designed so that they do not bend more than 1/360 of their length when a normal load is placed on them. Bridges are designed to bend less than half as much as floors. To find out what causes a floor—or a bridge—to bend, try the following project.

BRIDGE BASICS
Place the two tables about 50 centimeters apart. Use the C-clamps to secure one piece of knot-free wood between

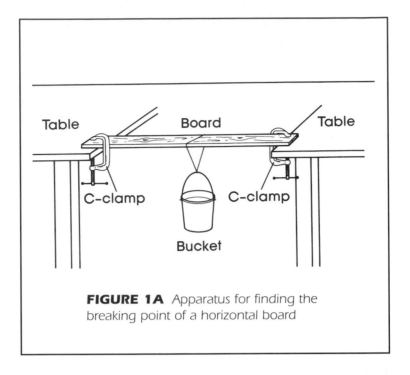

FIGURE 1A Apparatus for finding the breaking point of a horizontal board

the two tables. Make sure this wooden board cannot move. As you conduct the rest of this project, think of the wooden board as a bridge.

Use the rope to hang an empty bucket from the center of the board (see Figure 1A). Add sand to the bucket until the board bends downward 1 cm. Measure the weight of the bucket and sand on the bathroom scale. Record your findings in a notebook. Keep adding sand to the bucket until the wooden board breaks.* Take a new reading of the combined weight of the bucket and sand.

---

* If you have trouble finding wooden boards, you can do just the portion of the project that involves bending the wood 1 cm. You will still get good data, although it will not be as complete.

Repeat the experiment with the supports closer to—and then farther from—each other. Each time, find the weight required to bend a knot-free wooden board 1 cm and then the weight required to break it. Record your results in a notebook.

Next, set up your equipment as shown in Figure 1B. Support a knot-free wooden board between four wooden blocks clamped to the tables. Hang an empty bucket at the center of the board. Add sand to the bucket until the board bends downward 1 cm. Measure the weight of the bucket and sand on the bathroom scale. Record your findings in a notebook. Keep adding sand to the bucket until the wooden board breaks.

As before, repeat the experiment with the supports closer to—and then farther from—each other. Each time, find the weight required to bend the wooden board 1 cm

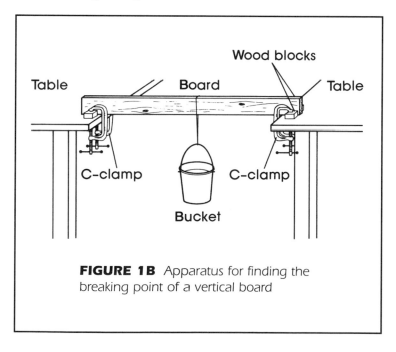

FIGURE 1B Apparatus for finding the breaking point of a vertical board

and then the weight required to break it. Record your results in a notebook.

Use a table saw to cut a wooden board lengthwise so it is half as wide (2.5 cm). *Caution: Table saws can be very dangerous. Do this step under adult supervision.* Place the cut board in the setup shown in Figure 1B. How much sand must be added to the bucket to bend the board 1 cm? How much sand is needed to break the board? As you record your data, be as precise as possible. Include the distance between the supports, the size and position of the applied force, the dimensions of the wood, the weight required to bend the board 1 cm, and the force required to break the board.

Are your results different with a full-length board and a half-length board? If so, can you explain the differences you see? How are force and the dimensions of the wooden board related?

You will find it easier to analyze your data if you enter it onto a spreadsheet. If you use Vernier Software's *Graphical Analysis* to graph your data, you will be able to find an equation that fits your data. See the Appendix at the back of this book for more information.

So far, you have been experimenting with knot-free wooden boards, but most boards contain some knots. A knot—the place where a tree branch meets the trunk—is a weak point. It compromises the strength of the board in the same way that a hole would.

To see this for yourself, carefully drill some holes in your wooden boards.* The holes should be at least 0.5 cm in diameter. *Caution: Drills can be dangerous.*

---

*Using wooden boards with real knots would not yield reliable results because knots vary in size and shape. For precise data, it is better to create artificial, uniform knots.

Make sure a knowledgeable adult is present when you do this step. Drill the holes carefully so that the wood does not split. Repeat the procedures described above with the "knotty" wooden boards. Remember to keep your data in a notebook or enter the information directly onto a spreadsheet.

Before you begin, develop a hypothesis that describes how you think the holes will affect the wood's strength. Do you think the location of the hole will make a difference? Does size matter? Drill holes in particular spots to investigate the first question.

Did your experimental results support your hypothesis? If not, revise or refine your hypothesis and do some more experiments. After you have found how the position of a knot affects the strength of a bridge, vary the size of the holes and repeat the experimental procedure.

Finally, you may want to try the experiment with wooden boards that contain real knots. Look for knots that are the same size as some of the holes you drilled. Be sure to test a number of boards with knots of equal size, because no two knots behave in exactly the same way. Compare your data from experiments with real and artificial knots. Are any of the results surprising? If so, try to explain them.

Doing More

- A device called a *cantilever* is often used to build porches. A simple cantilever is shown in Figure 2. Using what you learned by performing the previous experiments, design a porch using a cantilever that is safe and gives the largest floor area with the fewest construction materials. Develop a hypothesis for how far a board can be cantilevered and still be strong

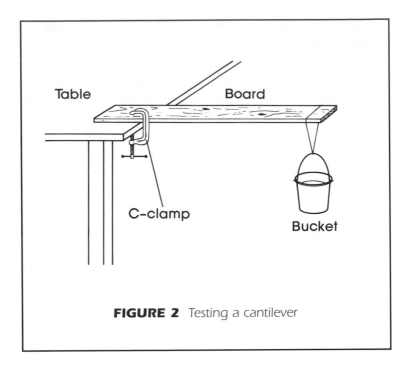

FIGURE 2 Testing a cantilever

enough to support a load, and design an experiment to test your hypothesis.

BUILDING MODEL BRIDGES

Once you know a little bit about bridges, you can begin to build scale models of more complex designs. Remember, though, that models may not always reflect real life. The relationship between size, strength, and weight is tricky.

Here's an example. Have you ever seen an ant carrying a piece of food that seems unbelievably large? An ant seems strong for its size, but if an ant were as tall as you are, it would immediately break its six legs and be crushed by its own weight. If an ant's size is doubled, its internal parts would have four times the cross-sectional area (length × width). As a result, the ant would be four times as strong. However, because weight is a function of volume (length × width × height), the ant's weight would increase *eight* times. Just imagine how much an ant would weigh if it was as tall as you are!

The same thing happens when a model of a bridge is scaled up to real size. A bridge that seems strong enough as a model may not be able to support its own weight when it is built full size. That's why models are useful for design, but materials or reinforcements may have to be changed before a life-size version is actually built. As you build your models, think about the bridges you have seen. Which designs are strongest? Which are the least expensive to build? Keep track of your findings in a notebook.

A *truss* is a structure of wooden or steel beams that forms a rigid framework. Many kinds of truss systems are used to build bridges. You can experiment with a variety of balsa wood truss systems to see which are the strongest. Make sure that the connections between the beams are strong so that they do not break before the

A truss bridge spans the Little Calumnet River
in Calumnet City, Illinois.

You can make a model bridges using lightweight wood, such as balsa wood, and glue.

beams do. Use glue to hold the pieces of balsa wood together. Small nails or staples will help hold the wood together while the glue dries.

Suspension bridges are popular because they can support large weights over long distances using a minimal amount of construction materials. Build a model of a suspension bridge to get a better understanding of how they work. Is a suspension bridge the strongest, most cost-effective type of bridge? Develop a hypothesis, and design an experiment to prove or disprove your hypothesis. Remember the scaling problems associated with models.

Investigate how a horizontal force, such as the wind, affects a bridge. After you have done a few experiments, try to design a bridge that is not affected by strong winds. Build a model to test your ideas. If your initial designs don't work out, don't feel bad. Sometimes professional engineers make mistakes too.

On November 7, 1940, a severe windstorm caused the collapse of the Tacoma Narrows Bridge, which crosses Puget Sound in Washington State. This disaster showed engineers that they did not completely understand the limits of suspension bridges. Do some research at your local library or on the Internet to find out more about why this bridge collapsed. Explain the role of a scientific principle called *resonance* in this terrible disaster. How did engineers design the second Tacoma Narrows Bridge?

Next, use what you have learned about building bridges to design the strongest possible bridge with a span of 2 m. Use balsa wood and string to build a model of the bridge. Test your model to see if it is as strong as you thought it would be. The Resources section at the back of this book lists some Internet sites and other sources that you may find useful.

Doing More

- As you learned earlier, the Romans used arches to build bridges. They also used arches and domes to build the ceilings and roofs of many buildings. Design

The Pont du Gard Bridge, which spans the Gardon River in France, supported an aqueduct that was a principal water source for the Roman city of Nimes. It is estimated that 44 million gallons of water flowed through this aqueduct each day.

and build some arches and test them for strength. Do some research at your local library or on the Internet to compare Roman arches to the Gothic arches used in many medieval cathedrals.

- In many cases, the principles used in the building of bridges are also used to construct houses. The floors and ceilings of a house are supported by the walls and foundation. In a sense, they "span" the distance between their supports. The boards holding up the floor are called joists. They must be strong enough to support the weight of furniture and people walking, dancing, or jumping up and down.

  Have you ever wondered exactly how a floor is built? In a particular situation, how do carpenters decide what size the boards should be? How do the boards react to various forces?

  To find out, construct a cardboard floor and observe how the spacing and board size affect its overall strength. How much sand can the floor support? Does the answer depend on the location of the joists or on the materials used to construct them? Talk to a builder in your area to find out what building codes allow and what they do not allow. Construct a model that follows the building codes.

DESIGNING CARS

FUEL EFFICIENCY: HOW EFFICIENT IS YOUR FAMILY CAR?

Engineers who design a car want to make sure that it handles properly and is comfortable for the passengers, but they also want to maximize its fuel efficiency. Many factors affect how much gas a car uses. A poorly tuned engine can affect a car's performance. So can snow tires, different kinds of weather, different drivers, wind, and the number of people and amount of cargo in the car. Cars driven mostly on highways usually get better gas mileage than cars driven primarily in heavy traffic.

By completing the following experiments, you can investigate some of the ways in which driving conditions affect gas mileage. These experiments may not be appropriate for a science fair, but if you analyze a car's fuel efficiency completely and support your conclusions with tables and graphs, it will make a good project for a class assignment.*

Begin by making a list of the various driving situations you wish to evaluate. These might include taking a trip of at least 160 km (100 mi) on a highway, driving around town, driving with the air conditioner on, and driving with the heater on. For each situation, keep track of how much gas is used, how far the car travels, how many people are in the car, weather conditions, and any other information you think might be important. Continue the experiment for about one month or until you have data from a number of tanks of gasoline.

For best results, driving conditions should be similar for each tank of gas. Try to fill the tank before and after a long trip so that highway driving and local driving can be evaluated separately. (Because short trips generally involve stop-and-go driving and idling at stoplights, they will probably require more gas than highway driving over a given distance. Also, the car must warm up each time it starts, which uses extra gas.)

Each time the tank is filled, make sure it is completely full. When the tank is almost full, foam sometimes causes

---

* You can do a lot with graphs if you know how to design them to your advantage. For example, if you want to show the difference in results for several cars that all get around 32 kilometers per 3.7 liters (20 miles per gallon), try setting the bottom of the graph at 28 km (18 mi) per gallon and the top at 35 km (22 mi) per gallon. This will allow you to see small changes. On the other hand, if you wish to show how similar the results are, try setting the bottom of the graph at 0 km (0 mi) per gallon and the top at 80 km (50 mi) per gallon. The resulting graph will be close to a straight line (see the Appendix). Keep this in mind the next time you see a graph used in advertising.

Which of these cars is more fuel-efficient—the single car traveling on the open road (top) and or one of the many cars traveling in the heavy traffic on the highway (bottom)?

the pump to shut off prematurely. (A sensor in the pump nozzle shuts off the pump when foam hits it.) Unless the person who is pumping gas is careful, the data you collect will not be accurate.

To find out how driving *speed* affects gas mileage, the car should be driven at two reasonably different speeds for a long period of time. If your family car does not have cruise control, the driver will have to make a conscious effort to avoid variations in speed. However, by checking the speedometer at regular intervals, you can get a good idea of how well the driver was able to maintain an average speed. Differences in gas mileage should be evident with speed differences of 16 km (10 miles) per hour if an entire tank of gas is burned.

To find out whether the wind influences a car's performance, wait for a windy day and then drive a few hundred miles into the wind. Drive the same roads on a windless day. On another windy day, drive a few hundred miles *with* the wind. Do you notice any differences in gas mileage? Explain your findings.

Investigate differences in gas mileage based on the amount of weight in the car. Do you notice a difference when one adult versus four adults ride a few hundred miles in a car? Be sure that the driver maintains the same average speed during both trips and that wind speed and other factors are similar.

If possible, evaluate several different cars. Ideally, the cars should be different sizes, and some should be significantly older than others. If you cannot do this yourself, look at the Environmental Protection Agency's website (*http://www.epa.gov/OMSWWW/*). It lists the estimated average gas mileage for many different kinds of cars and as well as information that may interest you.

INVESTIGATING AIR FRICTION

When engineers design cars, one factor they pay close attention to is *friction*—a force that opposes the motion between two objects or surfaces. When a car is moving, there is friction between the car and the air. To make a car more fuel-efficient, engineers look for ways to make the air flow more smoothly over the hood, roof, and trunk.

Have you ever noticed that most newer cars have molded, or *streamlined*, mirrors, while most older cars have larger, clunky mirrors? The newer streamlined mirrors reduce air friction, so the newer cars get better gas mileage. Many modern cars are so carefully designed to reduce air friction that even opening a window can increase the car's fuel consumption. Some car manufacturers say that using a car's air conditioner in hot weather takes less fuel than driving with all four windows open. Can you design and conduct an experiment to test this claim?

On the other hand, a roof rack reduces a car's performance because it interrupts the flow of air over the car. If suitcases or boxes are loaded on the rack, the car's performance is further reduced.

Air friction affects all moving objects. Its strength depends on the object's shape and the velocity with which air moves past it. When you pedal a ten-speed bicycle at 36 km (22.5 mi) per hour, about 90 percent of the energy you exert is lost to air friction. When you pedal at a rate of 7.2 km (4.5 mi) per hour, only about 4 percent of the energy you exert is lost to air friction. The best way to study air friction is by using a wind tunnel, which provides a stream of uniformly moving air. The following activity provides instructions for building and testing a wind tunnel.

BUILDING AND TESTING A WIND TUNNEL

What You Need	
Cardboard	Paper
Duct tape	Scissors
Fan, at least 50 cm in diameter, with two or three speeds	Permanent marking pen
	Four 1-inch nails
1-cm mesh wire screen slightly larger in diameter than the screen on the fan	Hammer
	Spring that stretches easily
Modeling clay	Spring scale
Wooden dowel, 1 × 40 cm	Stopwatch that measures fractions of a second
Wooden board, 15 × 30 cm	Ruler

Bend the cardboard into a long, round tube and tape it so that it holds this shape. Make sure the wind tunnel is at least four times longer than the diameter of the fan and that it does not vibrate when the fan is turned on. Place the wire screen about 30 cm from the fan to help reduce rotation of the air.

Use the modeling clay to build a model car or airplane about 8 cm long. Place the model at one end of the dowel, and fit the other end of the dowel into the spring. Choose a spring that stretches easily so that you can measure small differences in force. A 4-newton force should stretch the spring 10 cm. Nail one end of the spring to the board, as

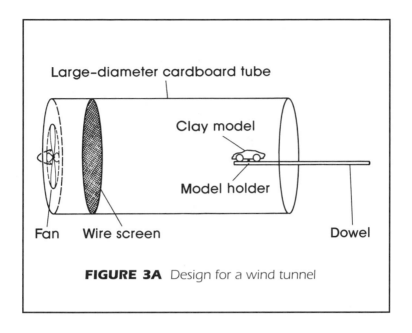

FIGURE 3A Design for a wind tunnel

Labels: Large-diameter cardboard tube, Clay model, Model holder, Fan, Wire screen, Dowel

shown in Figure 3A. To keep the wooden dowel in place, hammer two additional nails into the wooden board. Finally, place a piece of tape as shown Figure 3b.

Use a spring scale to calibrate the spring (see Figure 3b). Using the paper and permanent marker, design and

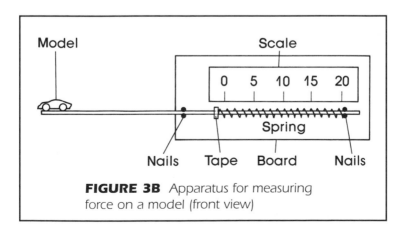

FIGURE 3B Apparatus for measuring force on a model (front view)

Labels: Model, Scale, 0 5 10 15 20, Spring, Nails, Tape, Board, Nails draw a scale that you can use to determine the amount of force exerted on the model. Or, to measure the force more precisely, you could use a force probe attached to a calculator or a personal computer.

When you turn on the fan, the air moving through the wind tunnel will exert a force on the wooden dowel and the model attached to it. Because you are interested only in the amount of force acting on the model, you must subtract the amount of force acting on the dowel from your results.

To measure the air speed for each fan setting, use the stopwatch to time how long it takes a small piece of paper to travel the length of the tunnel. Repeat this test several times and average your results. Divide the length of the tunnel by the average time it takes to travel the distance. Because it takes such a short time for the paper to travel down the tunnel, this method for measuring air speed is imprecise. Nevertheless, for this simple project your results will be acceptable. If you wish to measure air speed more exactly, you could use a photogate.

Now that you have a working wind tunnel, you can use it to investigate air friction. Determine the frictional force exerted on the model car at various wind speeds. After you have completed some tests with the modeling clay formed in the shape of a car, replace it with a lump of clay that is 5 cm in diameter and repeat the tests. Do you see a difference in the amount of frictional force?

Next, reshape the clay so that it has two cone-shaped ends. Place the clay on the holder so that one cone faces the fan and the other cone faces the wooden board. Do you notice any difference in the amount of frictional force exerted on the clay? Try rounding the ends of the cones so that the clay is shaped more like an egg. Now repeat the tests. Explain your findings.

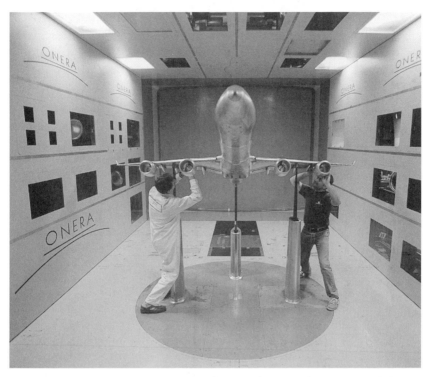

French scientists use a wind tunnel to see how a model of an actual airplane reacts to different conditions.

Air flows more smoothly over objects that are streamlined than over objects with rough edges. Scientists use the term *laminar flow* to describe what happens when air flows smoothly over an object. The opposite of laminar flow is *turbulent flow*. With laminar flow, air friction is related to an object's cross-sectional area—the area you see in profile—and the square of the air speed. With turbulent flow, the frictional force is greater. When frictional force is greater, more fuel is required to move a car—or an airplane—a given distance. That's why engineers try to design streamlined cars and airplanes.

Doing More

- Build a balsa-wood model airplane and test it in a homemade wind tunnel. Look at the model carefully and try to think of ways to make it more streamlined. Alter your model accordingly and retest it in the wind tunnel. Is the frictional force reduced?

- At a toy or hobby shop, buy a model of an old, square-shaped car and a model of a newer, more streamlined car. Build the models and test each one in a wind tunnel. Try to alter the older car so that its frictional force is similar to that of the more streamlined car. Be sure not to change more than one variable at a time.

  Compare the shape of a sport-utility vehicle or minivan to that of a sedan and develop a hypothesis to test which gets better gas mileage. Call a local car dealer or use the website given on page 30 to find out whether your prediction is correct.

- Tractor-trailer rigs, or "semis," use a lot of gas. Can you come up with a new design for these vehicles that

Large trucks carry heavy loads over long distances, and because of the rapid increase in the cost of gasoline, it is important that they be as fuel-efficient as possible.

would allow them to hold the same amount of cargo and be more fuel-efficient?

- For an airplane to take off, air friction—or drag—must be overcome by forward force—or thrust—from the engine. Modify your wind tunnel to measure forces at right angles (upward) to the flow of air and test a model airplane. How does the lift of an airplane's wings relate to drag?

  Study some of the designs in the books on paper airplanes listed in the Resources section at the back of this book. Design and build several different paper airplanes and test them in a wind tunnel. Can you modify the designs to create a plane that flies more smoothly and goes farther?

  Can you develop a way to test drag in moving water?* You could conduct some experiments in a swimming pool, a stream, or the ocean.

---

* Engineers often perform these kinds of tests to find the most efficient shapes for boats and submarines. Frictional forces are greater in water because water is more dense than air, but otherwise the principles are approximately the same. For some people, setting up an experiment in water may be easier than building a wind tunnel.

CHAPTER 4

ROCKETS AND RIDES: FORCES AND MOTION CAN BE AMUSING

HOW ROCKETS WORK

In the late 1600s, an English scientist named Isaac Newton developed three laws to explain the motion of objects on the ground and in Earth's atmosphere. Newton's third law tells us that for every action, there is an equal and opposite reaction. In other words, when something is pushed forward, something else must move backward the same amount.

For example, as you blow up a balloon, the air *pressure* inside it increases. If you let go of a fully inflated balloon, air rushes out in one direction. The balloon reacts by moving in the opposite direction. You can see the same principle at work if you hold a garden hose while wearing in-line skates. As a steady stream of water flows out of the hose, the recoil from the water will move your skates— and you—in the opposite direction. The faster the water leaves the nozzle, the faster you accelerate.

The exhaust of a rocket works exactly like that steady stream of water. The gas molecules that make up the exhaust are produced as fuel burns inside a rocket's engine. The forces of action and reaction, which propel the rocket forward, occur the moment the fuel is burned—before the exhaust leaves the engine. The movement of a rocket does not depend on anything outside the engine. In other words, a rocket is not propelled forward because its exhaust pushes against air.

This is an important idea because space is a vacuum—it contains no air. In space, there is absolutely nothing to push against. As a matter of fact, a rocket works better in space than it does in Earth's atmosphere because there is no air in space to get in the way of the exhaust. To learn more about how rockets work in Earth's atmosphere and in space, you could perform some experiments with a model rocket.

EXPERIMENTING WITH FUEL-BURNING ROCKETS

Some kinds of model rockets burn fuel. *Caution: These rockets can be very dangerous. Make sure a knowledgeable adult supervises your experiments with fuel-burning rockets. Follow the manufacturer's instructions carefully. Do not modify the rocket in any way, and use only the amount of fuel specified.*

Begin by examining how the amount of fuel used and the rate at which it burns affect the rocket's flight. You may have difficulty determining the rocket's final height. It will be much easier to measure the distance it travels from the angle of firing.

If possible, experiment with several kinds of fuel-burning rocket engines. Can you predict how differences in total *mass* and nozzle size will affect the rockets' performance? Try graphing some of the data you collected while conducting one of the previously described experiments

A student experiments with a model rocket.

you have completed. Graphing programs, such as *Delta-Graph*, can create colorful three-dimensional graphs.

To avoid the danger associated with fuel-burning rockets, you can use a software program called *CompuRoc*.* It simulates model rockets and shows you what happens when you make various modifications to the rocket and change the amount of fuel used.

* You can download this software from *http://www.mwn.net/info mac/sci/compu-roc-201.html.*

EXPERIMENTING WITH WATER ROCKETS

You might want to consider conducting experiments with a water rocket. They are safer and easier to use than fuel-burning rockets. Watching them blast through the air is more exciting than watching a simulation on a computer screen.

To operate a water rocket, all you have to do is add water and then pump air into it. When you launch the rocket, the air pushes the water out, causing the rocket to rise. Water rockets can be "refueled" quickly and, because they don't go as far as fuel-burning rockets, it's easier to measure the distances they travel.

You can buy a water rocket at a toy store, or you can make your own using a 2-liter soda bottle and a bicycle pump.* Begin by investigating the relationship between the amount of water and air pressure in the rocket's engine and the resulting flight time and distance. To do this, you need to measure the mass of the rocket, the mass of the water added, the height to which the rocket rises, and the air pressure in the rocket. Experiment with the water rocket to find the amounts of water and air pressure that make the rocket go no higher than you can measure easily.

If your rocket rises no higher than 5 m, collecting data will be relatively easy. To measure heights in this range, place pieces of tape every 0.5 m along a piece of rope and hang the rope out of a second-story window. When the rocket is fired, compare the rocket's altitude to the markers on the rope.

---

* For directions and experiment suggestions, see publication 501, *Rockets Away*, published by the Ohio State University Extension. Copies can be ordered by e-mail (*pubs@postoffice.ag.ohio-state.edu*) or by regular mail (Media Distribution, 385 Kottman Hall, 2021 Coffey Road, Columbus, OH 43210-1044).

To measure air pressure, find the maximum length of the pump stroke by pulling the pump handle out as far as possible and then measuring how far it can be *compressed*. The distance the pump lever moves is related to the volume of air inside. For example, pushing the pump in halfway reduces the volume of air by half, and pushing the pump three-fourths of the way in reduces the volume of air to one-fourth its original value. With one-half the volume, the pressure is doubled. With one-fourth the volume, the pressure is quadrupled. Use a tire gauge to find how many pounds per square inch equals one compression.

The valve on a water rocket is designed so that when the pressure in the pump is greater than the pressure in the rocket, air moves into the rocket. Therefore, you can measure the pressure in the rocket by finding the pressure at which air starts bubbling into the rocket. You can use the relationship between volume and pressure to make a pressure scale on your pump as shown in Figure 4. A bicycle pump is used to add air to a soda-bottle rocket, so you can use a standard tire gauge and obtain more accurate data.

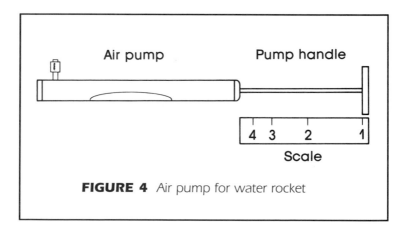

FIGURE 4 Air pump for water rocket

Most water rockets can hold only a small amount of water, so the air pressure inside the rocket does not change much as water is forced out. For the purposes of these experiments, the small change in pressure can be ignored.

Add a little water to the rocket and record that amount in a notebook or computer spreadsheet. Pump the rocket to a predetermined pressure and launch the rocket. How high does the rocket climb? Repeat this procedure several times to get an average value for the height. Be sure to use exactly the same amount of water each time.

Now repeat the experiment using a different amount of water. Try a few runs with less water and a few runs with more water. How do your results differ? Remember to keep track of your data. If you have entered the data onto a spreadsheet, you can use a graphing program, such as *Graphical Analysis*, to create a graph with the amount of water on the *x*-axis and the height on the *y*-axis. You can also use this graphing program to find an equation that describes the flight of the water rocket. See the Appendix at the back of this book for more information.

Doing More

- Do you think there is any relationship between the mass of the rocket and its maximum height? Develop a hypothesis and then design an experiment to test it. One way to increase the mass of the rocket is to tape weights to it.

- Try firing your rocket at an angle instead of straight up into the air. Does the rocket behave any differently? If so, why?

- Put a little dishwashing liquid in your water before you add it to the rocket. Does this change the way the rocket flies? What happens when you add olive oil to the water? By adding these liquids, you are changing the *viscosity* of the water. The viscosity of a fluid describes its resistance to flow. For example, molasses is a highly viscous fluid, while water is less viscous, and air is only slightly viscous. Develop a hypothesis that describes the relationship between viscosity and

When syrup, a viscous fluid, is poured
out of a container, it flows slowly.

rocket performance, and design an experiment to test your hypothesis.

Repeat your experiment using warmer and then cooler water. Next, try adding various amounts of sugar to the water. Try the experiment again but with a series of increasing viscosities. Use colder water or measured amounts of sugar to increase the viscosity. Be sure to record all your data and graph your results.*

- As your rocket shoots through the air, water is expelled in the opposite direction. How do you think the size of the water's exit hole affects the rocket's flight? To find out, you will need two rockets—one with a larger hole and one with a smaller hole. When all other factors are kept the same, how does performance vary? Graph your results.

- If you cannot get a second rocket, you may be able to change the size of the opening with a drill. *Caution: Drills can be dangerous. Make sure a knowledgeable adult is present when you do this step.* Test the rocket a few times before you start drilling, because once you increase the size of the hole, you cannot make it smaller again. By using a series of increasingly larger drill bits, you can see how changing the size of the exit hole alters the rocket's flight.

Be sure to keep track of all your data in a notebook or spreadsheet. When you have completed your experiments, graph your results. If you use a computer graphing program, such as *Graphical Analysis*, you can

---

* To find the viscosity of water at different temperatures and the viscosity of various sugar solutions, consult *The Handbook of Chemistry and Physics*. Ask your science teacher if you may borrow your school's copy, or look for the book in your local library.

find an equation to fit your data. See the Appendix at the back of this book for more information.

- Using what you have learned from your experiments, find the amount of water, the angle, the type of water solution, and the size of water exit hole that allow the rocket to rise the highest.

AMUSEMENT PARK RIDES

A roller coaster can make you scream with delight or feel sick to your stomach. Some parts of a roller coaster ride can make you feel as if you are falling uncontrollably. Roller coasters with loops cause you to experience the forces around you while you are upside down. A tilt-o-whirl spins you round and round until you are dizzy. It changes your rate and direction of rotation quickly. An octopus spins you around and then quickly pulls you horizontal, and it moves your body in unusual ways too.

Amusement park rides are fun—and sometimes scary—because they are designed to make you feel forces differently than you do in everyday situations. You can visit a local amusement park, experience some of the rides, and try to figure out what the engineers who designed each ride had in mind. Analyzing amusement park rides may not win you any prizes at a science fair, but these kinds of investigations can teach you a lot—and they are fun too!

As you try out a variety of rides, think about how they work and how they make you feel. Most of them make you experience forces associated with acceleration in unusual ways. You can measure these forces with the simple device shown in Figure 5. For example, if the spring scale measures twice the normal value required to support the mass, then the amusement park ride is exerting twice

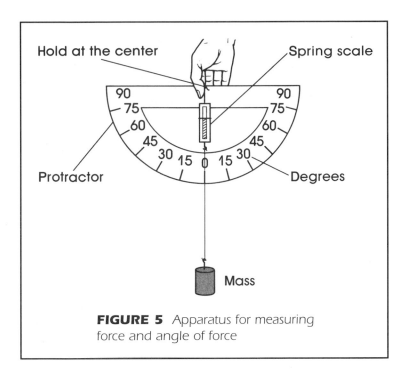

Hold at the center

Spring scale

90   90
75   75
60   60
45   45
30 15 0 15 30

Protractor

Degrees

Mass

FIGURE 5 Apparatus for measuring force and angle of force

the normal gravitational force on the mass—and on your body. Ask a math or physics teacher to help you use the angle that the string makes to the horizontal to calculate the horizontal force exerted by various parts of the ride.

Because gravity always pulls down on you, this force is considered "normal." When you accelerate downward, you do not feel as much gravitational force. Because it is different from what you are used to feeling, it seems strange. When you accelerate upward or in a circle, you feel more force than usual. Again, this difference seems strange to your body. Hop on a few amusement park rides and try to identify when changes occur with downward and upward force as well as with circular force, or *centripetal force*. Compare exciting or scary rides, such as a roller coaster, to rides that are not, such as a carousel.

For each ride, calculate the average velocity and acceleration. Compare those values to the velocity and acceleration of those parts of the ride that seem scary and those that don't seem scary. To measure velocity, check how long the ride takes to go a measured distance. To measure the acceleration, record the velocity at two points and divide the change in velocity by the time it took to change.

Finding the distances can be a bit tricky. You could measure your stride, or pace, before heading off to the park and then use your pace as a standard unit of measure while you are there. For a roller coaster, you could try counting supports and then measuring the distance between supports. *Caution: Be very careful when you do this. Be sure to obtain permission from the person who runs the park. The owner or operator might have the distances you need on file. Explain what you are doing to the person operating the ride.*

Measuring the height of a ride may be a bit more difficult. Ask your math or physics teacher how you can use a protractor to estimate the heights you need. Do this before you go to the park, so that you will be able to gather all the data you need while you are there.

If the ride turns, determine the radius through which it spins. Find out which spinning rides are most likely to make people sick, and then try to figure out why. Be sure to consider both the radius of the circle and the rate at which the ride spins.

To get the best possible data at an amusement park, use a precise measuring device such as a three-axis accelerometer connected to a Texas Instruments calculator. Ask your science teacher if this equipment is available at your school and if you may borrow it. If you collect data with this device, you can easily download it to a personal computer and create graphs that show which parts of a particular ride have the greatest accelerations. See the Appendix at the back of this book for more information.

Doing More

- You can measure "fear" by taking a person's pulse rate or blood pressure: first under normal conditions, and then while they are on an amusement park ride. *Caution: Before you do this, be sure to obtain permission from the person running the amusement park and the person operating the ride.*

    Ask your school nurse if you can borrow a simple device that measures a person's pulse rate. If not, check a medical-supply store or contact a company that manufactures these devices. They may be willing to let you borrow one for a few days.

    You may also be able to find a heart-rate device that you can hook up to a calculator. Some of these can be clipped to a person's earlobe; they detect minor changes in blood flow. Others must be taped to a person's chest; they measure the heart's electrical signals. The second kind of device will probably be more useful.

- As long as you are at an amusement park, why not take a look at the games. Can you analyze them to find out why they make money? Do some make more money than others? If so, why?

    If you try some of these games, you'll see that some are easier than others. While it is possible to win most of them, the odds are really against you in some of them. Also, be on the lookout for scams. Watch the operator's moves very carefully. Do you notice any tricks?

- Build a model of an amusement park ride. As you analyze the motion of your model, you can learn some

The roller coaster at Sea World on the Gold Coast in Queensland, Australia, is a "corkscrew" roller coaster.

interesting engineering principles. If you try to build a roller coaster, start with a single chute. Then add jumps, loops, and other features. If the roller coaster "car" jumps through the air, you can learn about projectile motion. If you design a loop, you can learn about centripetal force. Try to design kinds of loops and jumps that real roller coasters don't have. Figure out why these might work in your model, but not in a real roller coaster.

Try taking force measurements along the track and measure velocity at various points to see if the laws of physics describe the motion. You may also want to determine the efficiency of the roller coaster. Begin by determining its *potential energy* using the equation:

$$\text{Potential energy} = mgh$$

where m is mass in kilograms, g is the acceleration due to gravity (9.8 m/sec²), and h is height in meters. At the bottom of your final ramp, all the potential energy should be changed into *kinetic energy*, which can be calculated using the equation:

$$\text{Kinetic energy} = \tfrac{1}{2}mv^2$$

where m is mass in kilograms and v is velocity in meters/second.

If your model roller coaster were 100 percent efficient, the final vertical upturn at the end of your track would bring the car to the same height as the one at which it began. In other words, the energy at the end would equal the energy at the beginning. At the high point, the roller coaster is not moving vertically, and its energy is all in the form of potential energy.

CHAPTER 5

EXPERIMENTING
WITH SOUND

Some scientists and engineers focus their efforts on designing equipment or structures that magnify or absorb sounds. They work in the field of *acoustics*. Finding ways to make the music played in an orchestra hall sound even better or designing office spaces that are quiet requires a knowledge of how sound is produced and the biological mechanisms that allow us to hear it.

Scientists have tried to unlock the secret behind the incredible sound of Stradivarius violins. These stringed instruments were built by Antonio Stradivari in the late 1600s and early 1700s. He used the Latin form of his name—Stradivarius—on the labels of his instruments. He is generally acknowledged as the greatest violin maker who ever lived. No one has ever been able to duplicate the sound of his violins. And despite the efforts of scientists, no one knows why these violins make such beautiful

The violins made by Antonio Stradivari (1644–1737) are considered the finest ever made. Stradivari is believed to have made approximately 1,100 stringed instruments— mostly violins, but also some violas and cellos.

music. Some people think the key may be the placement of the sound post, which transmits sound from the top of the violin to the bottom, but no one has proved this. Other people think that it is the quality of the wood that he used. The wood came from old spruce trees, which is not available today.

INVESTIGATING SOUND WAVES

When a violin is not being played, its strings are straight and the forces acting on it are balanced. When you pluck a violin string, it moves away from its equilibrium position. A counter force then works to restore the string's equilibrium. The result is a vibration called a standing wave, which has *antinodes*—points where the string's displacement from the equilibrium is quite large—and *nodes*—points where no motion occurs.

The standing waves that form when you play a violin are similar to waves that form when you move a jump rope up and down. In fact, you can think of a jump rope as a long, very loose violin string. To see this for yourself, tie a rope to a stationary object. Hold the other end of the rope and move your hand up and down quickly. In what direction does the wave travel? How does the wave's direction of motion compare with the direction in which various areas of the rope move?

Ask a friend to take some photographs of you moving the rope. By placing the developed images side by side, you should be able to see nodes and antinodes. If possible, take some multiexposure photos of the rope. These should show the nodes and antinodes of the standing wave in a single image. Ask your art teacher or someone who works at a camera shop for assistance with this activity.

What happens when sound waves reach your ears? When a standing wave hits your outer ear, it is captured and sent into your external ear canal, as shown in Figure 6. It strikes your eardrum, a thin membrane, and passes into your middle ear, where it encounters three tiny bones that magnify the vibration. These bones transmit the wave to a fluid-filled structure called the cochlea in your inner ear. The cochlea passes the vibration to your auditory nerve, which carries the vibrational message to your

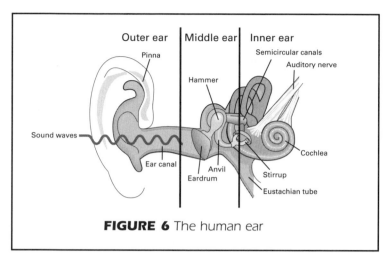

FIGURE 6 The human ear

brain. Your brain translates the message into the sound you hear.

This seems like a complicated process, yet it happens at lightning speed. That's why it seems as if you hear a violin's sounds at the same time that you pluck the strings.

Do you want to build your own musical instruments? You can examine waves produced by a violin, a guitar, or other stringed instrument by varying the amount of force exerted on a piece of vibrating kite string.

THE ACOUSTICS OF STRINGS

What You Need	
Door buzzer with power source	Wooden block
Table	Kite string
Two C-clamps	Small spring scale
	Tape

Clamp the buzzer to one side of the table with a C-clamp. Use the other C-clamp to hold the wooden block to the other side of the table. Tie one end of the string to the clapper (the vibrating part of the buzzer) and run the other end over the wooden block, as shown in Figure 7. Turn on the buzzer, hold the end of the string, and pull gently. As you slowly increase the force of your pull, you will see standing waves form and then disappear.

Attach a spring scale that can measure 10 newtons (2.2 pounds), or a computer force probe, to the string. Now you can measure the amount of force you exert on the string. Find the force required to make a standing wave with one antinode. How much force is required to make two, three, and four antinodes?

Change the length or thickness of the string and see what happens. Do you need more or less force to produce a standing wave? Be sure to record your data on a spreadsheet and plot your results using a graphing program, such as *Graphical Analysis*. See the Appendix at the back of this book for more information.

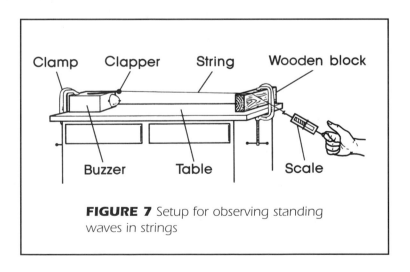

FIGURE 7 Setup for observing standing waves in strings

Can you find an equation to fit your data for each set of circumstances? Can you come up with an overall equation that takes all the factors into account?

Try to change the *frequency* of the buzzer. You may be able to do this by taping extra mass onto the vibrating part. If you can change the frequency, investigate the relationship between buzzer frequency and the amount of force required to make one and two antinodes.

Doing More

- Use a strobe light to determine the frequency of the vibration in the kite string. To do this, adjust the speed of the strobe light until you see a single string that is not moving. Find the frequency of the wave with one antinode and a given force. Then, keeping the force on the string the same, change the frequency of the buzzer until there are two antinodes. Find the new frequency of vibration.

  Repeat this for standing waves with as many antinodes as possible. Explain your results. After several trials, graph and analyze your results.

THE ACOUSTICS OF WIND INSTRUMENTS

Have you ever seen a clarinet, a flute, or a trombone? All these instruments contain a tube of air. When standing waves build up inside them, the instruments produce beautiful melodies. The following activity will give you a better understanding of the way many kinds of musical instruments work.

Roll the clear plastic into a tube just large enough for the speaker to fit inside. Tape the tube along the seam to make it airtight. Place the speaker in one end of the tube, and seal the end with tape. Cut a disk slightly smaller than the diameter of the tube, and use the nail to attach it to

What You Need	
Thin, clear plastic, 0.3 × 2 m	Wooden dowel, 1 m long and 0.5 cm in diameter
Cellophane tape	Table
Speaker, 5 to 8 cm	
Cardboard	Teaspoon of fine sawdust
Scissors	Audio oscillator that can produce a single frequency
Small nail	

the end of the wooden dowel. Make sure that the disk fits snugly inside the tube and can be moved back and forth by pushing or pulling the wooden dowel. Lay the tube on the table, and scatter the sawdust along its bottom. Connect the oscillator to the speaker with the wires.

Set the oscillator at a frequency of 600 cycles per second, and turn it on. Standing waves are forming in the tube, although you cannot see them. Air molecules at the antinodes are moving rapidly, while those at the nodes are not moving at all, and it won't take long for the molecules at the antinodes to begin pushing the sawdust until it rests at the nodes (see Figure 8).

Move the disk at the end of the tube in to shorten the length of the tube and watch the sawdust. Does a new pattern form? Next, move the disk out to lengthen the tube. Again, note any changes in the position of the sawdust. You should notice that even small changes in the length of the tube can make quite a difference in the sawdust pattern.

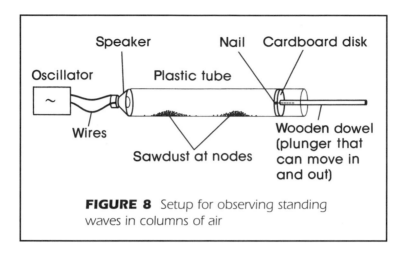

FIGURE 8 Setup for observing standing waves in columns of air

Change the frequency of the oscillator and repeat the same procedure. What effect does frequency have on the standing waves that form in the tube?

Adjust the frequency of the oscillator and the length of the tube until you create a standing wave with two antinodes. You will know that you have achieved this when you see two piles of sawdust. Double the frequency, and watch what happens. Finally, cut the frequency in half. What kind of sawdust pattern forms? Be sure to keep track of your findings in your lab notebook.

Doing More

- Using the tube apparatus, find the speed of sound in air. Adjust the frequency and length of the tube so that two antinodes are present and the wave travels the tube's length each cycle. The speed of sound is equal to the length of the tube (the wavelength) multiplied by the frequency:

$$v = f\lambda$$

where v is the speed of sound, f is the frequency in cycles/second, and λ is the wavelength in meters.

Can you think of other ways to measure the speed of sound? You could use sound sensors attached to a computer. Develop a setup that takes advantage of this equipment.

- Use the tube apparatus to determine the speed of sound in other gases. *Caution: Be sure to use small containers of gases that are not poisonous or flammable. Helium and carbon dioxide are good choices. Make sure the room is well ventilated.* The gas can be pumped into the tube at the speaker end. Generally, you must keep adding gas to the tube to replace what escapes.

- Find the speed of sound in other substances, such as water. What happens to the speed of sound above sea level? Why? Use a vacuum pump to measure the speed of sound in air at pressures of less than 1 atmosphere.

  You could extend your experiment by collaborating with a student who lives at a much different altitude.* You could also enter a collaborative project into a ThinkQuest competition. For more information about this contest, see Resources at the back of this book.

A LOOK AT MUSICAL INSTRUMENTS

The tones you hear when someone blows into a wind instrument are caused by white noise, or sound made up of many frequencies. The sound "ssssss" is similar to the

---

* For example, if you live at low altitudes, try using the Internet to contact a school in Denver, Colorado. See if you can find a student interested in repeating your experiment in this city's high altitude. See the websites *http://www.keypals.com* and *http://www.epals.com/*, which both contain information about contacting schools in various parts of the United States and throughout the world. Teachers and science fair judges will be impressed if you make the effort to collaborate with young scientists from other areas.

sound produced in the mouthpiece of a wind instrument. The white noise causes standing waves to occur in the column of air in the instrument.

Because only specific frequencies form standing waves, only specific frequencies or notes are amplified and heard. The size and shape of a column of air and the pressure of the "wind" determine the frequencies of the permitted standing waves and the *amplitude* of each frequency. Each instrument produces its own unique mix of frequencies. That is why you can distinguish between two different instruments playing the same note.

Building your own musical instrument can be interesting and rewarding, but you will need patience because instruments take time to build. As you experiment, you can learn a lot about sound waves and about how and why instruments produce the sounds they do. You could build an instrument by purchasing a kit or try making one from scratch. Or, if you're really ambitious, you could design and build a new kind of instrument. The following instructions will help get you started.

BUILDING A MUSICAL INSTRUMENT

What You Need

Small-toothed saw	Pliers
Wooden dowel, 30 cm	Modeling clay
Plastic pipe, 1 m, with an inner diameter of 0.5 cm	Small screwdriver
	Round file
Drill and drill bits	

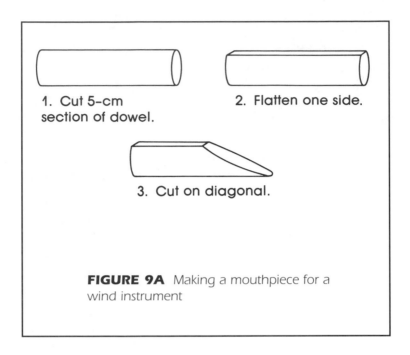

1. Cut 5–cm section of dowel.

2. Flatten one side.

3. Cut on diagonal.

FIGURE 9A Making a mouthpiece for a wind instrument

Use the small-toothed saw to cut a 5-cm section of the wooden dowel. *Caution: Make sure a knowledgeable adult is present when you use the saw.* Cut the dowel lengthwise so that it is flat on one side (see Figure 9A). Next, cut the dowel diagonally from the center to one end. Now you have a mouthpiece.

Use the saw to cut a 30-cm length of pipe. Cut a slit about 1 cm wide about 3.8 cm from one end. It should go through about one-fourth of the pipe's diameter. Push the dowel mouthpiece into the pipe so that its cut is centered under the slit. Use a small amount of modeling clay to seal any cracks between the mouthpiece and the pipe (see Figure 9B).

The small opening between the mouthpiece and the pipe will enable you to produce white noise. When you

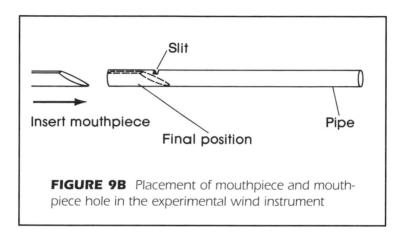

Slit

Insert mouthpiece

Final position

Pipe

FIGURE 9B Placement of mouthpiece and mouth-piece hole in the experimental wind instrument

blow into the pipe, air will rush through the small opening and hit the slit, and this moving air will produce a noise.

Try blowing gently through the pipe. Generally, blowing hard produces just noise, not a clear note. You may get a note at this stage of construction, but you will probably have to bend the pipe slightly to get a good tone. With pliers, bend the pipe right next to the slit on the side away from the dowel. First, bend it a small amount and see if you get a clearer noise. Then increase the bend until you get the clearest note. If you bend it too far and the note sounds worse, it may be possible to unbend the pipe with a screwdriver. The bending helps make the air flow properly.

Your instrument is similar to a recorder, an instrument that has a flutelike sound. If you are having difficulty getting a sound out of your instrument, you might want to look at a recorder mouthpiece to see what your mouthpiece should look like.

Drill a 0.5-cm hole halfway along the pipe. Use the file to smooth the inside and outside of the holes. Then place a finger on the hole and release it while blowing. The pipe should make a different note. Make sure you blow slowly to produce a good, clear sound. The harder you blow, the worse the result will be.

Once you have a hole that changes the *pitch*, determine which hole size produces the clearest sound. Vary the hole size but make sure the inside of the hole has no rough edges. Use a file if necessary. If you make the hole too large, put tape over it and start a new hole.

After you find the best hole size, place other holes of similar size along the tube until you can play a musical scale—a series of different pitches that make up an octave. Start by covering any holes you have drilled in the tube and call this note "do." Then, find a position for a hole for the note "re." Repeat for the rest of the scale—mi, fa, sol, la, ti, do. Cover any misplaced hole with tape.

It may take time to develop a complete scale. It is easiest to drill holes all along the pipe and then cover them all with individual pieces of tape. Then, starting with the holes at the end farthest from the mouthpiece, remove pieces of tape and see which holes make the proper pitch. Holes that don't make the proper pitch can be covered up again. Repeat the process until you have a scale.

When you have the proper hole placement, use a new piece of pipe, and drill holes exactly where the holes are that created a scale on your first experimental pipe. You have now built your own musical instrument!

Doing More
- Examine the effect of widening the end of the pipe in the musical instrument you have just made. The wide end of an instrument, such as a trumpet or trombone, is called a bell. Experiment with the shape of the bell by using either cones made out of paper or larger-

diameter pipe. What does a bell do to the pitch of your instrument? How would you "correct" the scale if the bell changed it? Pay particular attention to the "quality" of the sound that the bell produces.

Analyze the tone of such instruments as oboes and clarinets. What effect does the bell have? Use a sound program on your computer hooked to a microphone. Look at the change in wave shapes and frequencies. Can you change the shape of the wave on the screen to match the physical effect? See if you can design a better bell. How would you test it?

- After you have built one instrument, it is easier to build others. Investigate what happens with larger- or smaller-diameter pipe. Make some generalizations and predictions about what you observe. With enough trials, you will have enough data to graph and analyze to produce an equation using a computer program, such as *Graphical Analysis*. See the Appendix at the back of this book for more information. Test your ideas.

- Change the shape of the mouthpiece by using a small cup, such as those found on trumpets. See if this kind of mouthpiece improves the sound.

- Use different material for your pipe and observe the differences in sound quality. Try using plastic tubing, wood, or bamboo. Try some recorders made from plastic and wood. Which sounds better? Why? What is the difference in shape of the wave forms? Take screen shots for your project display.

- Design a stringed instrument with one or more strings, and build it. The string, instead of a column of air, provides a standing wave, which is then amplified by the rest of the instrument. In a guitar, the top,

This boy is playing an acoustic guitar.

which is usually made of wood, vibrates because the string does. This vibration creates the waves you hear as sound. Without the large motion of the guitar's top surface, the strings can hardly be heard. When you buy a guitar, you pay for the "box" (especially the top). You might be interested in buying a kit to build a dulcimer or other instrument. The instrument can be used for your own experiments.

- Build two stringed instruments and vary the construction methods. For instance, you might change the thickness of the top piece of wood or you might change the material used for it. Listen for differences in sound produced by the different instruments and record their wave shapes.

- Try using lengths of garden hose to make a buglelike instrument. By just varying lip pressure, a 2-meter length of hose gives many notes. What notes are being played? Why those notes? You can "tune" your instrument by cutting off lengths from the end. Try sticking a funnel into the end for louder music. Get several friends together and form a "rubber band." (Groan!)

- When you are familiar with the wave forms for several musical instruments as seen on your computer, try seeing if you can "picture" vowels. What is the wave form difference among such sounds as "ah," "ay," and "ee"? For a science fair project, use *Hyper-Card*, *AppleWorks* (formerly *ClarisWorks*), or Microsoft *PowerPoint* to play sounds and show their wave forms. Set up an oscilloscope with a microphone so that viewers can try their own voices. This can be an attention-getter. Many people are fascinated by their own voices.

WAVE PATTERNS: CHLANDI FIGURES

Chlandi figures—named after German inventor Ernest Chlandi (1756–1827)—are patterns produced by vibrations in flat pieces of material. For example, when such a material is vibrated by a violin bow, sand on a plate forms characteristic patterns. The patterns depend on the plate's shape, where the plate is held, and where the bow is rubbed.

The patterns occur because standing waves form in the metal. Standing waves form as the waves reflect back and forth in the plate. The waves in the plate can be thought of as ridges with crests and troughs, just like ocean waves. When two troughs or two crests reach the same spot simultaneously, the waves combine to make large waves and produce an antinode. Other places always have a crest and a trough present at the same time and produce a node.

Sand placed on the plate jumps around at the antinodes. It moves until it gets to a place where there is no motion—a node. Therefore, the nodes "collect" sand, and the antinodes "remove" it.

These patterns are fun to make, but they are also useful tools for learning more about how musical instruments make sounds. Chlandi patterns formed on the back of a poor-quality violin are irregular. By working with Chlandi figures, you can learn how wave patterns form in musical instruments. As a result, you should be able to build a better instrument. Here are some beginning experiments with Chlandi patterns.

MAKING CHLANDI PATTERNS OF VISIBLE SOUND

A violin bow can be purchased for $25 from a music store or you may be allowed to borrow one from your school's music department. (If you are careful, you won't harm the bow.)

Cut a square sheet of metal approximately 15 cm on a side. Attach the metal sheet to the corner of a large table with a C-clamp. The table should touch the sheet, or plate, at only one point. Shake sand onto the plate and rub the plate's edge with the violin bow. The sand will form patterns. Where are the nodes and antinodes? Record what you see with a drawing or a camera.

Next, investigate how different patterns form when the metal is rubbed in various places. Change the clamp's position along the edge of the plate and note the changes. Why did they occur? What changes have occurred in the standing waves?

Finally, drill a hole at the center of the plate and use a screw to fasten the plate to the wooden stick. Draw diagrams of the new patterns that form when the plate is rubbed in different places, and see if you can explain why they form.

Doing More

- Change the shape of the plate. What happens? Why do the nodes and antinodes form where they do? Try such shapes as a circle and a rectangle.

- Predict what happens if you use two clamps instead of one to support the plate. Do the experiment and explain the actual results.

- Try to predict what happens to the pattern when you make a specific change in the shape of the metal. Instrument makers change the shapes of their instruments in an attempt to make the standing waves larger, thus causing a louder sound. Test your predictions.

- A more complex project uses a loudspeaker instead of a bow to generate the standing waves. The speaker is attached to an audio oscillator. The oscillator allows a particular frequency to generate the standing waves instead of the random frequencies produced by the bow. Your science teacher may have an audio oscillator. The speaker does not vibrate a metal plate easily, so use a thin sheet of plywood or paneling 3 mm or less in thickness. Place the speaker in a small cardboard box, and rest the plywood on the box, as shown in Figure 10.

  You may need to amplify the output of the oscillator to give a large enough vibration to the wood. A stereo amplifier can be used if you are careful not to damage it. *Caution: Before you make any electrical connections, ask for the help of someone familiar with electronics so that you do not damage the amplifier or the oscillator.*

  Note the patterns on the piece of wood when a particular frequency is played through the speaker. Then change the frequency to twice the original value. Does the pattern change? How do the initial pattern and the pattern with twice the frequency compare? Make a small notch in the instrument. Is the change what you would expect?

  Cut the wood to form the shape of a violin or other musical instrument. Before you run the experi-

70

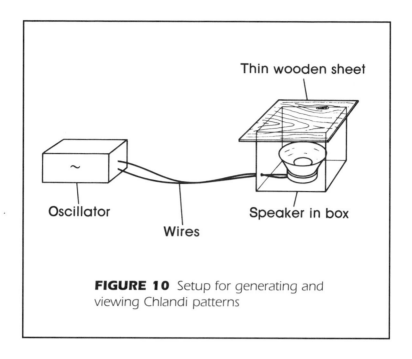

FIGURE 10 Setup for generating and viewing Chlandi patterns

ment, predict the patterns that should occur at various frequencies. Then see whether your predictions are correct.

- Start with a well-defined Chlandi pattern formed on one of your pieces of wood. Draw the pattern and then use sandpaper or a planer to make the wood thinner in some sections. Changing the thickness of the wood alters the way waves travel through that section. Should changes in Chlandi patterns occur? If so, what should they be?

- Try to predict the changes in Chlandi patterns that occur when you make certain variations in the shape or thickness of the wooden plate. If you are building a violin, for instance, it is desirable to have uniform patterns at all frequencies. This makes the instrument sound good at all frequencies. If you do not have such patterns, work to improve them.

- Although this project may take a long time, you can take your experiment with Chlandi figures a step further. You can build your own musical instrument, such as a guitar. As you work with the wood, make sure that the front and back of the guitar have uniform Chlandi patterns. If the patterns are not uniform, or strange patterns exist, sand the wood before you have invested a lot of time. Also, talk with an instrument maker who can give you many more suggestions.

SOUNDPROOFING

Noise is becoming an increasing problem in our environment. Engineers try to reduce noise by designing materials that absorb sound, thus making the environment quieter. Many factors affect how sound travels and how much noise reaches your ears.

Flat, hard surfaces reflect sound well and do not reduce noise. Sound-absorbing materials are generally soft or porous. Soft materials absorb sound, while porous materials reduce sound by trapping it in small holes. Fabric, for instance, is soft and porous; it is a good absorber when placed on walls. Another efficient material is common acoustic ceiling tile. Sound goes right through the many small holes in the tile and is lost in the area above—never to return. Why does a full auditorium absorb more sound than an empty one? People's clothes absorb sound and scatter it: the material has few flat surfaces. The scattered waves are less organized and thus less obvious.

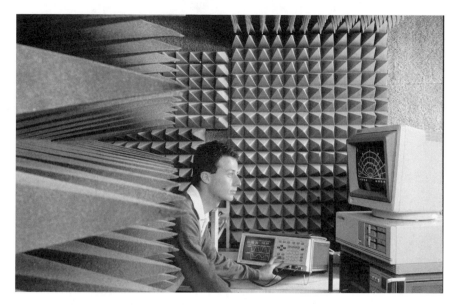

The soft, pointed materials in this soundproof room trap
sound waves, making the room soundproof.

Projects in sound reduction can be complicated, so
you may have to use equipment from your science department. However, some investigations can be done rather
simply. The following experiment involves the difference
in sound absorption in rooms of similar sizes. You will
estimate how much sound-absorbing material is in a room
and then gather data to see if the amount of material
affects the time it takes for a sound to fade away.

ACOUSTICS OF BUILDINGS

In a building such as a school, many rooms have the same
dimensions. If one room seems noisier than another, the difference is probably related to the quantity and type of sound-
absorbing material present. A room seems noisy if it takes a
long time for sounds to die out after they are produced.

What You Need

Several classrooms of similar size Stopwatch	Two blocks of wood that can be held comfortably, one in each hand

Examine a number of rooms and determine the amount of sound-absorbing material in each one. Consider various features, such as the number and size of wall hangings and the type of ceiling tile. Most likely, many rooms will have similar amounts of sound-absorbing materials, so you must look for extreme cases. For example, find two rooms with a lot of sound-absorbing materials, two average rooms, and two rooms with few sound-absorbing materials. This sample of six rooms is a bit small, but you can still obtain useful data.

In each room, have a friend make a "standard noise" by clapping two blocks of wood together. Use the stopwatch to measure the time it takes for the sound to die away. Have your friend make the noise at a distance from you to prevent the initial loud noise from hurting your ears and making it hard to hear the sound die away.

Timing must be done carefully. The time it takes for you to react to the sound must be the same in each trial. Otherwise, this "reaction time" will cause errors in your data. You can be quite accurate if you start and stop the watch according to a set standard. Start the stopwatch as a reaction to the noise and stop it when you hear no noise at all. Use a microphone and sound software, such as *LoggerPro* from Vernier Software, on a computer or calculator to make your readings more quantitative. This combination can also be used to obtain sound levels in units called decibels. See Resources at the back of this book for more information.

The differences between most classrooms is probably small, so you may have to set up some conditions. Test a room when all the room decorations have been removed for some reason—during vacation time, for example. In this way, you are looking at an extreme case. You can also try hanging extra curtains or tapestries in a room.

Doing More

- Using the methods described above, investigate the acoustic properties of your house. This project is easy to do if you are moving into a new house or apartment. In fact, echoes are one of the things that bother people in new homes or apartments. With nothing in the rooms, no sound is absorbed and noise reflects easily. Ask the following questions: With the bare walls, did the designer make the house quiet? How much of a change does adding the furniture make? Do any rooms have shapes that are not rectangular? Does the sound die away at a different rate in these rooms? Use a microphone and sound software to make your readings more quantitative and obtain sound levels in decibels.

  Tape recorders can also be used to measure sound intensity, because these machines have meters to measure sound intensity. When you use a meter, your standard noise should be the constant-volume noise produced by an amplifier and speaker. Either place the meter well away from the source so that the sound travels a long distance to the meter, or bounce the sound off the walls or ceiling so that it reaches the meter indirectly.

If you use a tape-recorder meter, you must calibrate it to obtain good results. Otherwise, it is hard to know when one noise is twice as loud as another. Talk with a knowledgeable person so that you can obtain reliable data with the equipment you have without damaging it.

- If you have a meter that measures sound intensity or a computer with the appropriate software, investigate soundproofing materials with more precision. Design your own materials and test them to see if they absorb sound efficiently. Your materials might be made of paper and cardboard with holes cut into them or they might be cardboard slats similar to those of Venetian blinds.

  Think about what materials absorb sound and what shapes make the sound become disorganized, both of which reduce its intensity. Place your standard source in one place and put your materials between the source and the measuring device. You might start working with materials similar to those sold as soundproofing materials and then expand your research with your own ideas.

- Study how auditoriums absorb sound by looking at the amount of sound-absorbing materials in them as well as their shapes and the way they are built. Build a model of an auditorium and trace the way in which waves travel from the stage to other parts of the auditorium. Build the wave tank (see Figure 18A in Chapter 6) and use water to make your model. It's much easier to see the waves and where they travel.

  Auditoriums may have places that trap sound and prevent echoes from coming back toward the front. Reducing the echoes prevents them from distracting both the audience and performers. One of the hardest places to perform in is a gymnasium with square concrete walls. The sound reflects back and causes problems for everyone.

Design a system that would make your gym quieter. The design should be inexpensive and it should look good too. Would changing the position of the bleachers help? What about hanging tapestries or flags? If possible, try out these ideas after getting permission from the people in your school. If you can make a gym quieter, why do sports arenas not do the same? Is the noise of the crowd a desirable thing to have at a game?

- What changes in shape can make a quieter room? Note that many auditoriums rise toward the back. This design is popular because sound waves tend to rise. As a result, sounds rise to the people in the back row. Sounds created by people shuffling their feet go over the heads of the people onstage, which makes everyone happy.

- Build an *anechoic* chamber (one that absorbs all sound). Try using different materials—egg cartons, cloth, cardboard, or foam. Investigate the properties of such a chamber.

- Perform a simple hearing test at your school with student volunteers. Hold a vibrating tuning fork near their ear, then on the mastoid bone directly behind the ear, and then on the top of the skull. Have each person fill out a questionnaire about how loud the sounds are at each of the three places. Some questions you might ask are:

  1. How many hours do you spend each day listening to music?

This tuning fork, which is vibrating at 128 cycles/second, generates sound waves. It can be used to test whether people can hear this particular frequency, or pitch.

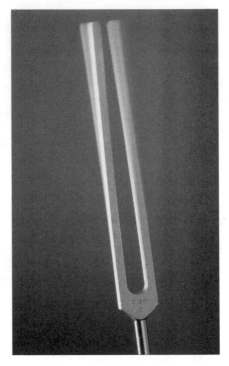

2. Do you wear headphones when you listen to music?
3. Do you play in an instrumental group?
4. Do you own a motorcycle?

Are there any other hearing-related questions you can think of? Compare the hearing levels of the students with their answers to the questions on your form, and use *Graphical Analysis* to see if you can find a correlation. See the Appendix at the back of this book for more information. At one high school, half the students couldn't "hear" the tuning fork on the skull by bone conduction. At an elementary school, the students and teachers could hear it easily. What can you conclude?

CHAPTER 6

A LOOK AT
LIGHT WAVES

Sound is not the only type of energy that takes the form of waves. Light can act like waves too. Projects that relate to light increase your understanding of the way light travels and interacts with objects. As you work on these projects, you will learn more about how light waves behave. Engineers who study light are working in the field of *optics*. These engineers use materials in new ways and try to design structures that transmit or absorb light waves more efficiently.

The following experiments are open-ended, and one question may lead to another. One of these questions may really fascinate you.

A PINHOLE CAMERA

It is possible to take pictures without a lens. A small pinhole in a light-tight box and film are all you require. You can use this equipment to take pictures and also to learn about the behavior of light as it passes through a small opening.

A pinhole camera is a very simple device, but it can actually take good pictures. One of the greatest American photographers, Ansel Adams (1902–1984), took one of his best photographs of Yosemite Valley with a pinhole camera. Although he used no lens, the photograph is equal in quality to that of his other fine photographs.

The critical part of taking photographs with such a camera is the pinhole size. If the opening is too large or too small, the picture seems out of focus. Ansel Adams had just the right-size opening. Experiment to find it.

The pinhole size is critical because of the way light waves behave. In a pinhole camera, a ray of light leaving a point on the subject goes through the pinhole (see Figure 11). It hits the film at a point that corresponds to the position of the object. With a large hole, a large circle of light appears on the film for each point on the subject. This causes a blurred image because the circles of light overlap.

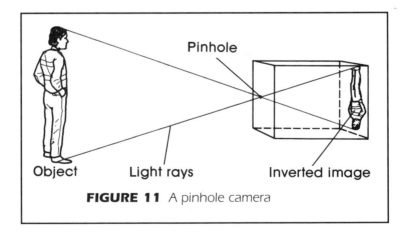

FIGURE 11 A pinhole camera

However, with a relatively small hole, the circle of light is small enough to make the overlapping of circles unimportant, although it does give a "soft" focus. Making the hole smaller than this optimum size causes *diffraction* to become important, and the circle of light gets larger.

The phenomenon of diffraction occurs when light waves go through a small opening and some of the light bends. With a very small hole, virtually all of the light bends or is diffracted, and the picture appears out of focus. With a slightly larger hole, a smaller percentage of light going through the hole diffracts, making the image clearer. Here are instructions for building a pinhole camera.

BUILDING A PINHOLE CAMERA

What You Need	
Shoe box	Pin
Scissors	Film
Masking tape	Darkroom or closet
Aluminum foil	

Use the shoe box as a light-tight box. Use the scissors to cut a hole 1 cm in diameter in one end of the box. Tape aluminum foil over the hole and poke a hole in the foil with the pin. Over the hole, place a small piece of tape that can be removed when a picture is being taken. Place the film at the other end of the box (see Figure 12).

The film should be at least 10×12 cm and can be either regular black-and-white film or Polaroid film. If you use regular film, you will need a large-size (120mm

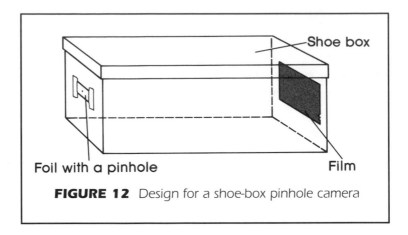

FIGURE 12 Design for a shoe-box pinhole camera

or 160mm) and must print your pictures from the negatives. This method gives good results. You will need a darkroom and a knowledge of darkroom techniques.

Use Polaroid film if you are not familiar with darkroom techniques. Obtain the kind of Polaroid film designed to be processed outside of a camera with special equipment. Ask your school's science or industrial arts department for this equipment, or try to borrow or rent it from a camera store.*

Once you have decided on a film type, construct a film holder for your box. Then load the camera in the dark, close and seal the box, and go to where you want to take your picture. Point your camera at a stationary subject, and make sure the camera does not move during the exposure. Remove the tape covering the pinhole, and at the end of the exposure, replace the tape over the hole and process your film.

Start with a hole the size of a normal pin. Initially try exposures of 10 seconds, 1 minute, and 5 minutes of an

---

*If the film is not available locally, try the website *http://www. freestylesalesco.com.*

outdoor scene to give you an idea of how your film and camera behave. Based on this research, vary the exposure time to get the optimum results. Remember, shorter exposure times allow less light in and cause a lighter negative, which results in a darker photograph. In the darkroom, it may be possible to get usable pictures even with improperly exposed negatives.

When you have obtained a good exposure on your film, try changing the pinhole size. Remember, the exposure must be shorter with a larger hole and longer with a smaller hole. Work toward finding the optimum-diameter hole and exposure time for your camera. A hole the size of a standard pin is just the starting point.

Doing More

- Try taking a picture of yourself. Because of the long exposure times, you can take a picture of a tree and then go and stand next to the tree to be in the picture! When you have exposed the film long enough, return to the camera and replace the tape. You must remain still for a long time to get a clear picture of yourself.

- Change the position of the film by moving it closer to the pinhole. What change occurs in the photograph? Shorten the exposure because the light from a larger area is falling on the film. Does the change in the photograph agree with what you would expect?

- What happens if the film is put into the box at an angle or in a half circle? Can you create special effects using this technique? What causes the changes that occur?

- Make a study of pinhole size versus picture clarity. Match pictures equally out of focus because the pinholes are either too large or too small.

A pinhole in a piece of aluminum foil can be an "instant magnifier" by allowing you to bring your eye much closer to an object. What does this say about your eye, pinhole size, and picture clarity?

LENSES

Lenses are used to focus light—in your eye and in a camera. However, no single lens can focus all colors of light at the same point. A given lens bends different colors of light in slightly different ways because each color has its own wavelength. Blue light has a shorter wavelength than red light, and the lens bends shorter wavelengths more than longer wavelengths. As a result, blue light and red light are focused in different places.

Ideally, camera lenses are built so that rays of light coming from the object are all focused at a corresponding point on the film. Because a single lens focuses different colors at slightly different places, camera lenses are

Different camera lenses allow photographers to take pictures from a variety of distances.

designed by using a number of "elements," or separate lenses. This combination of elements allows all the colors to be focused at the same place.

Seeing how lenses affect light is an interesting project. Easy projects utilize glass lenses. Other projects involve building your own lenses and seeing how they behave. Lenses can be built out of glass, but it takes a long time to grind the glass. An easier method uses supplies found in chemistry storerooms and hardware stores. Building your own lens allows you to investigate how light behaves in materials of your own choosing. In this experiment, you will use a glass lens to investigate how it focuses different wavelengths of light.

OPTICS OF LENSES

What You Need	
Scissors	Putty
Two file cards	Lens (thicker in the middle than at the edges)
Masking tape	
Wire screen, 5 × 5 cm	
Small light source, such as a 15-watt bulb in a socket	Meterstick
	Colored filters

Cut a hole 3 × 3 cm in a piece of file card 10 × 12.5 cm, and tape the wire screen over the hole. This screen acts as the object. Mount the light source and use putty to mount the file card with the wire screen, lens, and the other file card for the screen in a straight line as shown in

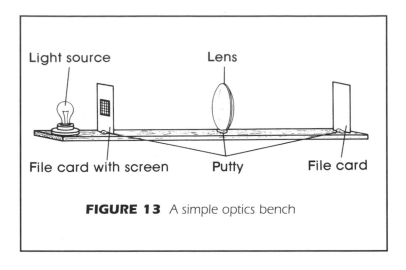

Light source　　　　　　　Lens

File card with screen　　　Putty　　　File card

FIGURE 13 A simple optics bench

Figure 13. You must be able to move all the parts easily and measure distances between the parts precisely. You need at least one red and one blue filter (for short- and long-wavelength light). You can buy these filters at a camera store or from Edmund Scientific. See Resources at the back of this book for more information.

Now experiment to find the focal length of your lens. During the day, hold your lens near a wall across from a window in a darkened room. Move it away from the wall until an image of the outside forms on the wall. Measure this distance, which is called the focal length of the lens (see Figure 14).

Again, in a darkened room, set up the light source, object, and lens so that the distance to the object from the lens is about twice the focal length. Place the screen on the other side of the lens from the object, again about twice the focal length from the lens (see Figure 15). Then move the screen back and forth until an image of the wire forms on the screen. If you do not get an image at first,

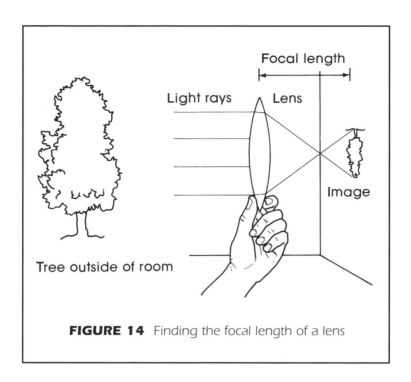

FIGURE 14 Finding the focal length of a lens

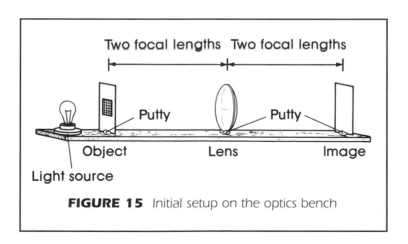

FIGURE 15 Initial setup on the optics bench

make sure that the object, lens, and screen are in a straight line and that the lens is mounted perpendicular to the line connecting the object and the screen.

The positions of objects and the images created by the lens are related to the focal length by a simple equation:

$$1/f = 1/D_o + 1/D_i$$

where f is the focal length, D_o is the object distance, and D_i is the image distance. Check to see that the object and image distances for your lens are related to the focal length as the equation predicts. Using a spreadsheet makes calculations easier. Graphing your data should give a smooth curve. See the Appendix at the back of this book for more information.

Next, try using the colored filters and see where the new focal point is. The difference in position for the focus is small, about 2 percent of the length, but it is measurable if you make the sharpest image possible. Once you have built the apparatus used in the first experiment, you are ready to build your own lens.

LENS ASSEMBLY

What You Need	
Two watch glasses (shallow, curved pieces of glass)	Water
	Grafting wax or silicone sealant
Small bucket or mixing bowl	

First, build a lens using the two watch glasses. Place them in a bucket of water with their concave sides together so that there is a hollow cavity. Make sure no bubbles remain in the watch glasses. Seal them under water with grafting wax, which retains its sticky properties even when wet. Grafting wax can be found in garden-supply stores. *Hint:* Cooled boiled water eliminates dissolved air and cuts down on bubbles.

Find the focal length of the lens by using the method discussed in the previous experiment. Now, mount your lens in the same way the lens was mounted in the previous experiment, and find the position of the image. Are the object and image positions for your lens predicted by the formula involving focal length? What happens when light of different colors goes through your lens?

Doing More

- Examine how lenses made of other materials affect light. Vary the optical properties of your lens by using different sugar solutions to fill the watch glasses. Make a few solutions with varying amounts of sugar, including a completely saturated solution (one in which you cannot dissolve any more sugar). This provides you with quite a range of optical properties.

  Change your concentrations in a series, graph the focal point versus the concentration, and make an equation for your data with *Graphical Analysis*. See the Appendix at the back of this book.

  You can also try using unflavored gelatin. This substance will add protein molecules instead of sugar molecules and be easier to handle after it solidifies.

- Work with lenses with different sugar solutions and look for the different positions of the white, red, and blue foci.

- Use watch glasses of different curvatures to examine how lenses of varying curvatures affect the focal length and foci of red and blue light.

- If you design camera lenses with all the colors focused at the same spot, you will need to work with what are called diverging lenses. Diverging lenses are thinner in the middle than at the edges and do not form an image in the same way as converging lenses—the lenses you have been working with.

  To form an image with your apparatus, you need to have two lenses, one converging and the other diverging (see Figure 16). Also, the optical properties—the strength of the sugar solution—must be different for the two lenses. Build a diverging lens in the same way as a converging lens, but use a watch glass

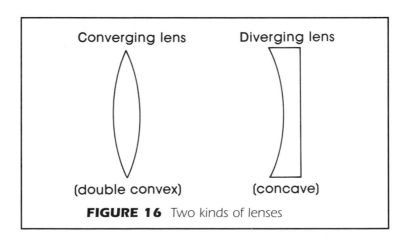

FIGURE 16 Two kinds of lenses

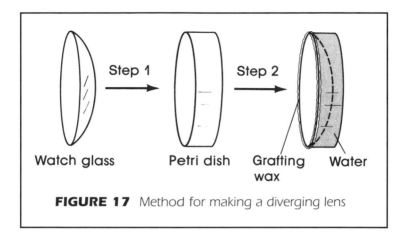

FIGURE 17 Method for making a diverging lens

and a small, flat dish called a Petri dish. Place the watch glass so that the center of the lens is thinner than the edges (see Figure 17).

With the diverging lens made with water, use white light to investigate where the image forms when both the converging lens with a sugar solution and the diverging lens are used. (If the diverging lens is too thin in the middle, you may get no image.)

Examine where the red and blue foci are for various combinations of diverging and converging lenses. By varying the sugar solutions, work toward having the red and blue foci closer together than their positions with one lens alone. Such a combination makes a better camera lens.

Note: As you work on this project, you will probably want to find out more about lenses. The "lens maker's equation" can be used to design a lens with a particular focal length.* You can do these

* This equation appears in many physics textbooks.

projects without any idea of why lenses behave as they do, but you will have a better understanding of the projects and make quicker progress if you learn more about optics.

WATER WAVES

Everyone has made waves in a bathtub, so we have all done some minor experiments with water waves. You can also use a bathtub, or similar-size tank, to do some simple but more scientific experiments to learn how waves form, move, and disappear. By working with waves, you can learn how harbors can be made safer and what makes a "fast" swimming pool.

Harbors are designed to prevent large, dangerous waves from entering. Jetties or ocean breakwaters—long structures projecting into the water—are often used to break the force of ocean waves. They make areas behind the jetty safe from the waves' energy. In swimming pools, swimmers move more slowly if large waves are present. Consequently, fast pools are designed to prevent waves from reflecting off the sides. Generally, the wave tops fall down into a gutter and are lost, reducing the reflected wave to almost nothing.

You can build a wave tank and run experiments to design ways to reduce the size of waves. Models placed in the tank are used to test your hypotheses about how to eliminate waves. The tank can also be used to investigate how standing waves develop in a body of water. Here is a beginning experiment in which you build a wave tank and model harbor to test what is required to protect the harbor from large waves.

THE PHYSICS OF WATER WAVES

What You Need	
Saw	Paint or varnish
1 sheet of CDX plywood, ½ inch × 4 feet × 8 feet (this contains waterproof glue)	Caulk (waterproof, like that used around bathtubs)
Nails, 1½ inches long	Sand of uniform size, pebbles, bricks, and other obstacles, such as blocks of paraffin
Hammer	
Waterproof wood glue	Scrap boards

Cut a piece of plywood 1.2 × 1 m for the base of your tank. Cut sides 30 cm tall to make a box—the wave tank. Use nails and glue to attach the sides to the bottom. When the glue is dry, paint or varnish the tank. Use the caulk to make the tank watertight (see Figure 18a).

Now you are ready to experiment. Move your tank to a place where you can fill it and test it for leaks. Do this in a place where water can be spilled without causing damage. A driveway is an ideal place for this experiment. Remember, you must dump the water at the end of your experiments. Plan ahead.

Fill the tank with 5 cm of water and build a harbor of your own design. You might start with a small semicircular bay. Make waves using a small board placed in the water and rapid back-and-forth motion as shown in Fig-

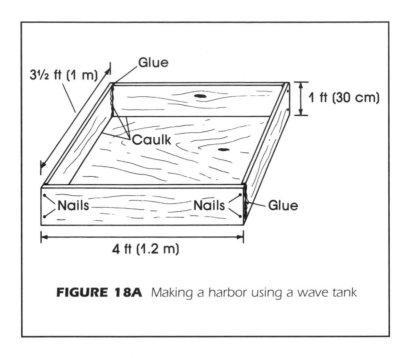

FIGURE 18A Making a harbor using a wave tank

Labels within figure: 3½ ft (1 m), Glue, 1 ft (30 cm), Caulk, Nails, Nails, Glue, 4 ft (1.2 m)

ure 18B. Remember you are making a model of a harbor, and make the waves to scale.

Observe how the waves travel into the harbor and affect the shore. You might put small model boats in the water and see how they move. Make the waves come from a variety of directions because real harbors experience waves from many directions during the year. Remember the "time squared" rule of relating models in motion to life size.

Next, with pebbles and sand, build a jetty or two to protect the harbor from storm waves, and test to see if your jetties protect the harbor. Build your jetties so that boats can get in and out of the harbor safely without bumping into one another or the jetties. Make waves

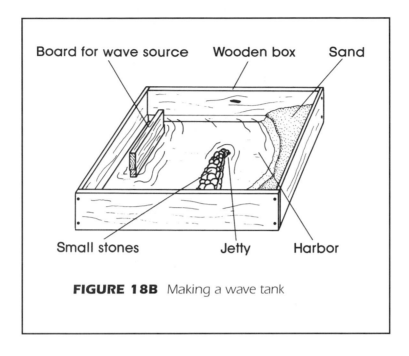

Board for wave source   Wooden box   Sand

Small stones   Jetty   Harbor

FIGURE 18B Making a wave tank

come from all possible directions. The jetties should protect the harbor from waves coming in any direction.

Doing More

- Is it possible to build jetties that prevent beach erosion? First examine beach erosion by making waves come onto a sand beach from various angles. Large waves are needed to cause erosion. What happens to the sand taken off the beach? Where does it go? Then construct jetties that prevent such erosion. Can all beaches near the jetty be saved? Is there any way to adjust these jetties for unusual wave patterns, such as those that showed up during the El Niño years of 1997–1998?

- Make the bottom of your harbor vary in depth. Generally, the main channel is deep and other sections are shallow. See how this affects the way in which waves strike the shore. Does the same placement of jetties work for a harbor of varying depth? Investigate the estuary systems of natural harbors that are not constantly dredged.

- Change the depth of water in your harbor as would occur with changing tides. Sometimes, during storm surges associated with hurricanes, tides are many feet higher than normal. Do jetties prevent damage when the water level rises?

- Build a mechanical wave machine that can repeatedly produce the same size waves. Build it so that the wave size can be changed. You can get small motors from Edmund Scientific. (See Resources at the back of this book.) Because you are using water, try to use one a motor that operates on batteries instead of more dangerous house current. ***Caution: If you use a motor that is plugged into the wall, get one that is specifically designed for use in water.*** With this machine, examine how destruction of the shore is related to wave height. Measure the differences of shore loss and wave heights and graph them. Can *Graphical Analysis* make a good equation for it?

- Sometimes it is desirable to have no waves reflected from the edge of a body of water. Fast swimming pools are designed this way, because any reflected wave makes it harder to swim. Use your wave tank to test ways to prevent any reflection of waves. Remember, swimming pools have vertical sides.

- Remove everything from the wave tank and examine how a sloshing wave acts in the tank. This kind of wave can develop in a bathtub, a swimming pool, or a larger body of water—in any container that you cannot tip over. Lift one end of the tank and watch the wave you create move to the other end. Then lower your end and the wave sloshes back. By moving the tank at the proper time, you can create a large wave. The water must be displaced to cause the wave. Experiment to see if the time for the sloshing wave to move down and back is related to depth. Find out if waves of other frequencies also produce large-amplitude waves.

- Try making a large-amplitude wave in a bathtub by lifting yourself out of the water at varying frequencies. Which frequencies make large waves? Which don't? How does the depth of water in the bathtub change the frequency? Gather enough data to predict the *period* of a wave in a swimming pool. Some pools now have "wave pools"; if you can find one, determine whether your predictions fit one of these pools. The period depends on the depth and length of the pool.

CHAPTER 7

A PHYSICS
OLYMPICS

In 1975, Dr. Robert Lillich had the idea of a physics olympics and held the first one at Indiana University of Pennsylvania. Since that time, many such events have been held. At a physics olympics, teams develop individual approaches to solve problems, and then test their methods. The most successful design, scoring the most points, wins.

Physics olympics projects are simpler than those we have discussed in this book, but they are educational as well as fun. A classic event in a physics olympics is the egg-drop competition. This event involves using a given set of materials to design an apparatus that will prevent an egg from breaking when it is dropped from a specified height. You can work on these designs by yourself, but it is more fun to compete with others. You might want to organize a physics olympics at your school.

When engineers try to solve a problem, they develop a hypothesis and build an apparatus that allows them to test the hypothesis. Then they experiment to see if their hypothesis was correct. In a competition, many events require you to do this in a limited amount of time—a few minutes or a few days. Arriving at a solution requires you to use your intuition as well as your scientific knowledge. The competition allows you to see the results of your work quickly and compare your ideas with those of others.

RUNNING A PHYSICS OLYMPICS

If you are interested in organizing a physics olympics, you will need the help of a teacher. The teacher can help you work out the format with other teachers and the school administration. Your job will then be to organize the people to help run the events. The combination of students and teachers can make the event run smoothly.

Keep a few guidelines in mind when you run a physics olympics. You need a list of events, a place to hold the competition, and a method of scoring to determine the winners, judges, and prizes. If you arrange all these things in advance, the events will run smoothly and will be fun for everyone.

Before you run a physics olympics, you must decide on the scale of the event. You may want to involve just your own class, or all the classes in your school, or all schools in a particular area. For a large event, entrance fees can help cover costs and provide prizes, as well as give you an estimate of the number of participants in advance. Knowing how many people will attend is helpful. Of course, the smaller the event, the easier it is to plan and run.

The event must be well planned, with clear rules. The rules will tell students what materials can be used and what determines the winner, as well as list any limitations on construction methods, sizes, or other features. These limitations may seem artificial, but real engineers must always keep limited budgets and limited technology in mind in their designs.

For example, in an egg-drop event you need to specify the materials that can be used, the maximum dimensions for the device that holds the egg, the height from which the egg is dropped, the surface used for landing, how the device is dropped, and what constitutes a broken egg. Without specific rules, the results may be ambiguous and competitors will be unhappy. The materials should be inexpensive and easily available.

Each event must take place in an appropriate location. For instance, a windy area is inappropriate for apparatus that might fall over in a slight breeze. There must also be sufficient space for both the contestants and onlookers so that people won't bump into one another.

Judges are needed to score and run the events. However, they do not need to be scientists because the things they judge are measurable. A judge's duties may include launching paper airplanes, dropping an egg apparatus, or measuring the height of structures. The judge's job is relatively easy and can be fun, but the judges must be decisive. Their decision should be final.

Physics olympics may have special software for scoring, as does the more general "Odyssey of the Mind," which also often involves construction projects. However, a computer spreadsheet can produce results quickly, and with no mathematical errors, to inform participants of all scores. Designing the spreadsheet is a good project itself—it clarifies how the competition is going to be scored. Prizes might be extra credit, award certificates, or trophies.

SAMPLE EVENTS

THE EGG DROP

In this event, an egg carrier is constructed to protect an egg from breaking when dropped. Many versions of this event are possible. The egg must fall freely from a given height and must not crack. The surface may be cement. After each drop, the team may repair the container, but they can add no material other than that provided.

- The container must be made from the three pieces of paper and 30 cm of cellophane tape provided. It must be able to pass through a square opening no more than 15 cm on a side. If not, teams can build a parachute and the egg can drop from any height. The vertical dimension, measured when the container is falling, may be larger than 15 cm.

- A 20-cm-long strip of paper, which is also provided, should be attached to the container. The judges hold this paper and release it for each trial.

- When you are ready to compete, you receive a raw, medium-sized egg. The judges drop the eggs from a height of 0.5 m and increase the height in 0.5-m intervals. Contestants should give the judges any special instructions for dropping the container before the eggs are dropped.

- The judges determine if any cracks have developed in the egg. The team that constructed the container that prevents an egg from cracking after falling the longest distance is the winner. For this, they receive 100 points. The other teams receive points in proportion to how their result compares with that of the winner.

A SLOW BICYCLE RACE

In this event, contestants ride a bicycle over a given course, taking the longest, rather than the shortest, time. The course is flat, 10 m long and 0.5 m wide, and clearly marked.

- The bicycle has one speed and a coaster brake activated by reverse pedaling. The bicycle must start from rest and keep moving forward at all times. During the ride, no part of the body may touch the ground. Hitting a marker disqualifies the contestant.

- Each team is allowed one practice ride and then has two attempts for competition. In the second round, the team order will reverse with the last going first. The team that takes the longest time to complete the course receives 100 points. The other scores are expressed as a ratio of the winning time.

Doing More

Other possible projects suitable for a physics olympics include the following:

- From a list of construction materials, contestants build a bridge that supports the largest weight spanning a given distance. It could also be scored by dividing the weight supported by the mass of the bridge, which encourages use of less than the maximum amount of material. The bridges can be built before or during the competition.

- With five similar blocks, contestants design and build a cantilever system that has the largest overhang. The blocks can be placed in any way to produce the desired effect.

- The contestants build airplanes from specific materials and then fly the planes for distance, accuracy, or a combination of the two.

- With a given set of materials, contestants build boats that support the greatest weight or can be propelled the longest distance by an energy source, such as a rubber band. Aluminum foil and straws are good building materials.

- Contestants build vehicles from various materials. The vehicles can be designed for speed, distance, ability to travel in a straight line, or ability to haul loads up a hill. The engine could be rubber bands; heat sources, such as a candle; or wind.

- Contestants build waterwheels that can do the most work as 1 liter of water falls a distance of 5 cm onto the waterwheel.
  - In this classic event, contestants build a paper tower as tall as possible with a given set of materials, typically a few sheets of paper and a given length of tape.
  - With various masses placed on a meterstick, contestants predict the position of the balance point in a given amount of time. Calculators may or may not be permitted.

- With a given set of materials, contestants produce the largest temperature difference in a given amount of time using solar energy. This apparatus might be built before the competition.

CHAPTER 8

SCIENCE
FAIRS

Entering a project in a science fair can be a rewarding experience. When you know you must make a presentation, you are forced to look at your project critically and to ask yourself questions about your data and conclusions. After all, it can be embarrassing when someone points out a flaw in your reasoning or asks a question you cannot answer. If you do not analyze your data thoroughly, you will not win a prize.

Science fairs are often sponsored by schools and local organizations. Each science fair has its own rules and specifications, so read the entry form and application carefully before planning your project. Projects that win at local competitions are usually entered in regional, state, or even national competitions. The last step is the Intel International Science and Engineering Fair, or the Intel

Science Talent Search, which is held annually at various locations throughout the United States.

A science fair project is judged on the basis of originality, presentation, and scientific content. Other people may have done projects similar to yours in the past, but yours should have a new viewpoint or a better method for collecting data. You must also show that you understand what you did and show that your conclusions are based on sound principles and good data.

Your project will be viewed by many people, so make sure it answers questions likely to be asked by students, teachers, parents, and judges. Clearly state what you did, show your data in a logical manner, and indicate how you

Students can participate in a science fair, such as the Intel Science Talent Search, with a project that relates to physics, mathematics, or engineering.

reached your conclusions. Preparing for a science fair seems like a lot of work sometimes, but in the end it helps you to learn more from your project.

THE PRESENTATION

Prizewinning science-fair projects never consist of just a paper. You need to have something to catch the judges' attention. Create a clear, colorful presentation. If your display includes something that the viewer can do, it will be a hit.

Using computer programs, such as *PowerPoint* or *AppleWorks* (formerly *ClarisWorks*), can help make your presentation more organized and interesting. These programs allow you to present your arguments point by point, create clear tables and graphs, and include sound and animation. It is also possible to have the presentation run automatically and continuously.

If you do this, make sure someone is always in charge of the computer equipment so that it doesn't get damaged or stolen. You also need a large computer screen so that more than one person at a time can see the presentation.

DESIGNING AND DOING THE PROJECT

Here is the process you should follow as you develop and conduct your project.

1. Choose a topic that interests you.

2. Do some research to come up with a project idea.

3. Think of an original hypothesis.

4. Design an experiment to test your hypothesis.

5. Conduct the experiment.

6. Organize your data in tables and graphs. Look for any results that seem strange or inconsistent.

7. Make sure your conclusions are supported by your data. If there are other ways to interpret your data, state them and show why your interpretation makes more sense.

8. Ask a friend, family member, or teacher to look at your data. Does the person have trouble understanding your graphs or the way you have explained your data? If he or she is confused, try to make your presentation clearer.

9. Write a report that consists of:
   - a title page with the name of your project, your name, school, address, and the date

   - an acknowledgments section in which you thank the people who helped you or let you borrow equipment

   - a table of contents

   - a statement of purpose in which you describe what you were trying to show

   - an abstract that allows readers to quickly find out what you did and what you found. Here are two examples:

     Changes in Viscosity with Various Soap Solutions
     The viscosity of soap solutions was investigated and the concentrations of the solutions were related to the viscosity. Viscosity was determined by measuring the flow rate through tubes. Viscosity decreased and then increased as a result of increasing the ratio of soap to

water. Both pure-soap solutions and pure water had a higher viscosity then combinations of water and soap.

The Consistency of Ski Wax and
Friction of Various Temperatures
The physical properties of ski waxes were studied and then related to the amount of sliding friction on skis. Different properties allowed the minimum friction at different temperatures. Apparatus was built to test the frictional force while the ski was moving at a constant speed and a force equal to that of an average skier was exerted on the ski.

- a background section that contains the information you found at the library or on the Internet as well as a basic explanation of relevant scientific principles

- a procedure that explains how you conducted the experiment. This section should include a description of the apparatus, including photographs and drawings if possible.

- a results section that shows your data clearly. Graphs and tables may help present the information effectively.

- a conclusion that describes what you found when you analyzed your data

- a bibliography that lists books, articles, and other sources you used

SPREADSHEETS AND GRAPHING

Back in the "ancient history" of the microcomputer world—about 1978—two people developed a program called *Visi-Calc*, the first successful spreadsheet program. It mimicked something the business community had been using for years.

Spreadsheets used to be big sheets of paper marked off in a grid that were used for holding information. For example, department stores used them. The names of the individual departments were listed down the side, and the days of the week ran across the top. The amount of sales per day went into each box. At the end of the week, adding up all the numbers in a row across would tell you the amount of sales for that department for the entire week. Adding up all the numbers in a column would give you the total sales for all departments on a particular day.

From this spreadsheet, a manager could add more columns to obtain other useful figures, such as sales per square foot of floor space in each department, or the expense of salaries per unit sales. Although the information was great for planning, the calculations involved were tedious. The advent of computer-generated spreadsheets made things a lot easier.

Scientists and students can use spreadsheets to make calculations and graphs much easier to use. For example, consider the weight of some boys on a middle school football team and some values used to find the standard deviation, which is a statistic used as a measure of variability.

In Table 1, notice how each number or column title now has a particular letter and number associated with it. The column heading "Weight (pounds)" could be referred to by saying "what appears at the intersection of column B and row 1." The weight of player 5 could be referred to as "B6." (There are 11 players but 12 row numbers.)

To make up this table, it isn't necessary to sit down with a calculator or a pencil and paper and figure everything out by hand—it can be done on a computer. The computer can calculate all the values in columns C and D, and then you can do a "copy" and

TABLE 1: Using a Spreadsheet to Find Standard Deviation

Row Number	A	B	C	D	E
1	Player	Weight (pounds)	Average Weight	Actual Weight— Average Weight	Value in Column D Squared
2	1	185	190.4	−5.4	29.16
3	2	230	190.4	39.6	1568.16
4	3	130	190.4	−60.4	3648.16
5	4	178	190.4	−12.4	153.76
6	5	267	190.4	76.6	5867.56
7	6	137	190.4	−53.4	2851.56
8	7	187	190.4	−3.4	11.56
9	8	177	190.4	−13.4	179.56
10	9	201	190.4	10.6	112.36
11	10	212	190.4	21.6	466.56
12	11	190	190.4	−0.4	0.16

"paste." You don't have to type in "190.4" eleven times. Just do it once, and then "copy" and "paste" it into the rest of the row.

On this spreadsheet, if you click your mouse on "cell" C2, then type "= B2 − C2," press <return> or <enter>, the answer "−5.4" appears. If you copy that cell and then paste it into the rest of the D column, all the answers come up immediately. To obtain the E column, you need to click in cell E2 and type "= D2 ∗ D2." On computers, the asterisk (∗) is used for multiplication.

You can probably find a spreadsheet easily at home or at your school. Many all-in-one programs, such as *AppleWorks* (formerly *ClarisWorks*), *Microsoft Works*, *WordPerfect Works*, *GreatWorks*, and others, have a built-in spreadsheet module. In programs such as *Microsoft Office*, an associated spreadsheet, such as *Excel*, means that each program can "talk" to the others. You can do all the calculations you need and then "cut" and "paste" the resulting table into a word-processing document.

Most spreadsheet programs have a graphing program or module associated with them. Separate graphing programs have more flexibility and more available types of graphs. Usually, for the all-in-one programs, you just highlight a section of your spreadsheet and then choose a graph type. The graphing module makes the graph for you. It's easy.

But you have to make sure you have chosen a graph type that is suitable for your data and your intended audience.

Table 2 is an example of a graph of the population of a particular species of fish in an area over several years. In the graph

TABLE 2: Number of Trout in Big Creek

Year	Number of Trout
1989	458
1990	510
1991	580
1992	470
1993	520
1994	600
1995	490
1996	560

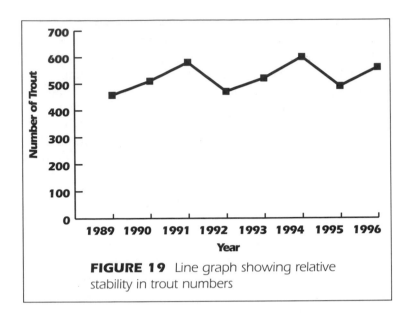

FIGURE 19 Line graph showing relative stability in trout numbers

shown in Figure 19, a line graph, the computer has "chosen" its own format. Notice that the graph seems to indicate that the population of trout in the creek seems to stay about the same value each year. What happens if a different range of values is chosen for the *y*-axis?

If the graphing program is "forced" to use 450 as its lowest value and 600 as the highest point, look what happens (see Figure 20). Notice that by choosing the range closer to the range of the data, the changes in the trout population look much more impressive. Don't forget that how you present your data can be as important to your science project as the data itself. Was your purpose in doing this fish count to show that Big Creek has had a stable population over the years you studied? Or was your purpose to show that Big Creek suffers from drastic fish kills every 3 years?

If you use a more advanced graphing program, such as *DeltaGraph*, you can generate very spectacular, three-dimensional graphs (see Figure 21). They certainly look impressive in science fairs, but do they show what you want to show? What

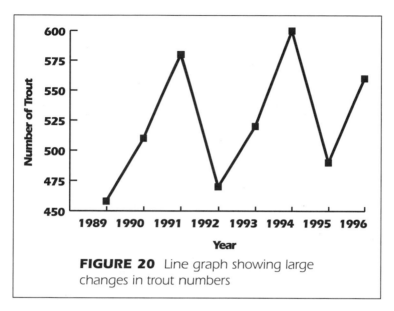

FIGURE 20 Line graph showing large changes in trout numbers

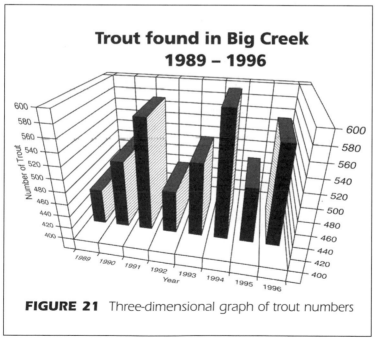

FIGURE 21 Three-dimensional graph of trout numbers

about bar graphs, pie charts, or histograms? Graphs should make it easier to interpret your data and they should also help a person looking at your report or science fair exhibit to understand your findings readily. You need to make decisions about what you graph, how you graph it, and what type of graph you use. What is it that you want to show?

Finally, besides making your data easier for both you and others to understand, some graphing programs add an additional refinement. *Graphical Analysis* by Vernier Software not only plots data as you input the numbers, but it can also generate a mathematical formula for the resulting graph. For example, if you charted the growth of yeast cells, you might get an equation that has an exponential term in it—a value that is squared or cubed. If you were looking at a more complicated line on a graph, the program might give you a quadratic equation that fits just that line—perhaps something like $y = 1.367x^2 + 3.8x - 1.8$. See Resources at the back of this book for more information.

Not only does a mathematical equation allow you to calculate results more easily (especially if you're using a spreadsheet), but having an equation in your report or science project will also impress your instructor. It won't attract most people who stop by your science fair display, but the judges and any mathematicians or scientists who view your setup will know you're doing the real quantitative work that scientists do.

GLOSSARY

acceleration—the rate of change of velocity per unit of time

acoustics—the study of sound—its production, transmission, reception, and effects

amplitude—the height of a wave; half the distance between the crest and the trough

anechoic chamber—a sound-testing chamber with no echoes

antinode—the point on a standing wave that marks the largest displacement from the equilibrium position. See *node*.

cantilever—a strut attached at only one end, such as a diving board

centripetal force—the inward force that keeps things moving in a circular path

compression—a pushing force

diffraction—the bending of light as it passes through a narrow opening that is close to its wavelength in size

force—the physical quantity that can affect the motion of an object (a push or pull). It is measured in newtons or pounds.

frequency—the number of vibrations, oscillations, or cycles per unit time

friction—a force that opposes motion when two bodies are in contact with each other. "Wind resistance" is a frictional force that is termed "drag" in aircraft.

hypothesis—a plausible solution to a problem; a guess used in an experiment conducted to verify or discard a solution

kinetic energy—energy possessed by an object in motion. See *potential energy*.

laminar flow—smooth flowing of a fluid or gas without turbulence. See *turbulent flow*.

mass—a measure of the amount of material; a fundamental physical quantity. Mass is not the same as weight.

mechanics—the study of how things move, how forces affect motion, and the forces exerted on all structures

node—the point on a standing wave where no motion occurs. See *antinode*.

optics—the study of light

period—the time for one complete cycle, vibration, revolution, or oscillation

photogate—a small optical probe connected to a computer that emits a small light beam. Whenever the light beam is interrupted, a signal is sent to the computer. A photogate can be used to measure the time it takes for objects to move past a particular point.

pitch—a sound caused by a particular frequency

potential energy—energy that is the result of the position of an object in a gravitational, magnetic, or electric field. See *kinetic energy*.

pressure—force per unit area; units may be pounds per square inch, millibars, or dynes per square centimeter.

qualitative—an observation that tells what is happening or how, but not how much. See *quantitative*.

quantitative—an observation that measures how much of something, compared to a known standard. Quantitative observations are "3.68 meters in length" or "a pressure of 14 pounds per square inch." Physicists try to make as many quantitative observations as possible because they are more useful in predicting things later. See *qualitative*.

resonance—strong vibrations of an object caused by sound frequencies that are the same as the natural frequency of the object

scientific method—the process scientists use to test and evaluate an idea

speed—how fast an object is traveling. Speed is usually expressed as distance divided by time—meters per second or miles per hour. See *velocity*.

streamlining—having a smooth outline that allows air to take the shortest path from one point to another

truss—a frame, generally of steel, wood, or concrete, built from components under compression and tension, as in a truss bridge

turbulent flow—air fragmented by friction with objects. Eddies result from turbulent flow. See *laminar flow*.

velocity—speed in a particular direction

viscosity—resistance to flow; fluid friction. For example, tar has a higher viscosity than molasses, which has a higher viscosity than water.

weight—the gravitational force acting on a mass in a particular gravitational field. (Your weight changes from planet to planet, but your mass stays the same.)

RESOURCES

BOOKS

Adams, Richard C., and Robert Gardner. *Ideas for Science Projects*. Danbury, CT: Franklin Watts, 1997.

Adams, Richard C., and Robert Gardner. *More Ideas for Science Projects*. Danbury, CT: Franklin Watts, 1998.

Adams, Richard C., and Peter H. Goodwin. *Physics Projects for Young Scientists*. Danbury, CT: Franklin Watts, 1999.

Agruso, Susan, Carole Escobar, and Virginia Moore. *The Physics Olympics Handbook*. College Park, MD: American Association of Physics Teachers, 1984.

Appel, Kenneth, John Gastineau, Clarence Bakken, and David Vernier. *Physics with Computers*. Portland, OR: Vernier Software, 1998.

Benade, Arthur. *Horns, Strings, and Harmony*. New York: Dover Publications, 1992.

Boy Scouts of America. *Model Design and Building*. Irving, TX: Boy Scouts of America, 1993.

Brisk, Marion. *1,001 Ideas for Science Projects*. New York: Prentice Hall, 1994.

Caney, Steven. *Steven Caney's Invention Book*. New York: Workman, 1985.

Ching, Francis D.K. *Building Construction Illustrated*. New York: John Wiley & Sons, 1991.

DeCamp, and L.S. deCamp. *The Ancient Engineers*. New York: Ballantine, 1988.

Derry, T.K., and Trevor I. Williams. *A Short History of Technology*. New York: Dover Publications, 1993.

Eastman Kodak Company. *Photography in Your Science Fair Project*. Rochester, NY: Eastman Kodak, 1985.

Friedhoffer, Robert. *Physics Lab in a Hardware Store*. Danbury, CT: Franklin Watts, 1996.

Friedhoffer, Robert. *Physics Lab in the Home*. Danbury, CT: Franklin Watts, 1997.

Friedhoffer, Robert. *Physics Lab in a Housewares Store*. Danbury, CT: Franklin Watts, 1996.

Friedhoffer, Robert. *Physics Lab in a Supermarket*. Danbury, CT: Franklin Watts, 1998.

Friedhoffer, Robert. *Toying Around with Science: The Physics Behind Toys and Gags*. Danbury, CT: Franklin Watts, 1995.

Levy, Mathys, and Mario Salvadori. *Why Buildings Fall Down: How Structures Fail*. New York: W.W. Norton, 1994.

National Science Teachers Association. *Science Fairs and Projects: Grades 7–12*. Arlington, VA: National Science Teachers Association, 1990.

Salvadori, Mario. *Why Buildings Stand Up: The Strength of Architecture*. New York: W.W. Norton, 1994.

Salvadori, Mario, Saralinda Hooker, and Christopher Rayes. *The Art of Construction: Projects and Principles for Beginning Engineers and Architects*, 3rd ed. Chicago: Chicago Review Press, 1990.

Simon, Seymour. *The Paper Airplane Book*. East Rutherford, NJ: Viking, 1976.

Stine, G. Harry. *Handbook of Model Rocketry*, 7th ed. New York: John Wiley & Sons, 1994.

Tocci, Salvatore. *How to Do a Science Fair Project*. Danbury, CT: Franklin Watts, 1997.

Vazquez, Laura. *Not Just Another Science Fair: A Handbook and More for Science Fair Organizers*. Glenview, IL: Scott Foresman, Goodyear Books, 1999.

Walker, Jearl. *The Flying Circus of Physics with Answers*. New York: John Wiley & Sons, 1988.

INTERNET SITES

Access Excellence

http://www.accessexcellence.com

Take a look at the "What's News" (science update), "Let's Collaborate" (online projects), and "Activities Exchange" (activities-to-go) sections.

Intel International Science and Engineering Fair

http://www.sciserv.org/iisef.htm

The Intel International Science and Engineering Fair (ISEF) is the Olympics, the World Cup, and the World Series of science competitions. Held annually in May, the Intel ISEF brings together more than 1,000 students from 40 nations to compete